P. M. Bikelés

AN INTRODUCTORY COURSE IN ARGUMENTATION

BY

FRANCES M. PERRY

INSTRUCTOR IN ENGLISH IN WELLESLEY COLLEGE

———o•o:❉:o•o———

NEW YORK ·:· CINCINNATI ·:· CHICAGO

AMERICAN BOOK COMPANY

To

KATHERINE BATES

PREFACE

An Introductory Course in Argumentation has grown out of my need of a text-book presenting the subject of brief-drawing and argumentative composition in so elementary a manner as to make it practical for a short composition course for college freshmen. My endeavor has been to simplify the subject to suit the understanding of students in the first years of college, or the last years of secondary school, without lessening its educative value.

In the first place, the student is practiced in the processes of argumentation without the added difficulty of research. No teacher of narration begins his work by demanding that a student write a historical romance requiring serious preliminary study of the period in which it is placed — he begins, rather, with simple pieces of work exercising the student's power of imagination on material that lies within his experience. The beginner in the study of argumentation should, in like manner, be set to work to exercise his reasoning power on familiar material. This is not a loss, but a gain. Even advanced students, when allowed to write at the start on subjects upon which they must "read up," develop little power to argue; they too often count their work done when they have gathered from a book and summarized the arguments of another. The student required to argue on material already at his command finds pleasure in turning it over, seeing it in new lights, in new relations, with new significance, and argument seems to him serviceable and pleasant work. I do not, however, advocate suiting endeavor to power, and at the close of the course the student is instructed in methods of research with the expectation that he will be ready to encounter added difficulties.

The subject is further simplified by leaving *persuasion* out of consideration until the student understands *conviction*. This, too, is a gain; the student who begins by suiting his argument to the hearer too often comes to value sophistry above thoroughness and accuracy; like a sharp bargainer he prides himself more on a fraudulent victory than on an honest one. With him specious reasoning and "bluff" are at a premium, and to outwit and circumvent his antagonist by fair means or foul, to "make a case," is his unscholarly ideal. The student whose interest is first enlisted in making a strong argument, can afterward be brought to see the importance of presenting it with tact and economy, without danger of confusing sound argument with mere tricks of oratory.

The instructor will find that simplification has been

effected without evasion of difficulties. While the course is intended to be as simple as possible, it is not intended to permit any otiose imitation of the form of argument without the substance. The difficulties are not slighted; they are taken by easy stages, and every point is clinched by drill in exercises hard enough to stimulate the average student to vigorous work. The two methods in use in teaching argumentation, the brief-drawing method and the syllogistic method, naturally assist and complement each other. My aim has been to combine these methods so that the one will help the student to understand the other.

While the course calls for a sustained piece of work, its preparation and criticism by installments are provided for, so that there is no dearth of work during the course and no accumulation of work at its close.

A good course in elementary argumentation should be introduced into every high school composition course. There is no form of discourse that will do so much to break a student of hand-to-mouth writing and thinking, that will so give him the habit of looking beyond his nose, of doing work in a purposeful way, with a sense of the relation of parts, of the structure of the whole composition. It facilitates development out of the acquisitive, transmitting stage into reflective, modifying, originating power.

Acknowledgment is due Messrs. Houghton, Mifflin & Company for permission to use certain copyrighted material; also to the Century Company for the selection from N. S. Shaler's *American Highways;* to Charles Scribner's Sons for the selections from Thompson Seton's *Wild Animals I have Known*, and Richard Harding Davis's *Gallegher and Other Stories;* and to Small, Maynard & Company for the selection from Mrs. Charlotte Perkins Stetson's *In this Our World*.

CONTENTS

THE PURPOSE AND THE USES OF ARGUMENTATION

THE purpose of argument is to make others believe as we believe. It is not enough, however, to strive to reach that end by assertions — we argue only when we offer reason and evidence to sustain our assertions. To argue, then, is to seek to establish the truth or the falsity of a proposition or statement by means of evidence.

This is for none of us an untried field of endeavor. Ever since we have had preferences we have tried to persuade others of their rationality. As children we were not content to announce to our mothers that we wished to go to a neighbor's house to play; most of us were eloquent in adducing reasons for the wish; "because" is a word with whose use we have long been familiar.

The type of the trained arguer is the lawyer, who makes it his chief study and practice to bring others to think as he wishes them to think. But the leader in any walk of life, if he would control the thoughts and actions of others, needs to be, to some extent, master of the professional advocate's art. Daniel

Boone, persuading his old neighbors to face the hardships of the frontier; Morse, urging upon capitalists the feasibility of the electric telegraph; Lincoln, proclaiming to voters that the Union could not exist half slave and half free; Charles W. Eliot, advocating the elective system in education, — such men as these have had to convince and persuade. Even one who has no great cause to advocate and no aspiration to influence others must in the simplest social and business relations frequently employ argument, pronounce an opinion and give reasons for it. Do you like your instructor's method of teaching German? Do you prefer Monday or Saturday for a holiday? Who is your candidate for class president? Who is your favorite novelist? Do you believe in co-education? These are questions that can not be disposed of with monosyllables. We are expected to know our own minds, to have views on many subjects and to be able to account for them. "Because" is in disrepute not because of the mental process it implies, but because the word so often exists with little or none of the argument of which it is the sign to justify it.

The need to argue is not confined to specialists, but the ability to do so in a clear, convincing way where the subject-matter is complex usually belongs only to those who have had special training in the process of argumentation. The tools demanded are

familiar — exposition, description, narration; the use
to which they are put is, as we have seen, familiar.
But the purposeful selection of just what is needed
to prove a proposition, and the effective organization
of it into an argument, call for a breadth of view, a
power of inference, and a sense of relationship that
rarely exist without cultivation.

Perhaps more important than the arguments we
enter into with others, are those inner debates that
arise over conflicting duties, policies, and pleasures,
and must be settled before no audience outside of
ourselves: Shall I tell the truth though it injures my
friend? Shall I go to the theatre when my mother
disapproves? Shall I give this beggar money? Shall
I do this work which I do not care for because it
pays well? Our own peace of mind and much
besides may depend on our ability to gather and to
weigh the evidence on both sides of questions such
as these.

The process of reasoning is useful to us not only
in shaping our own course of action and in influenc-
ing others, but it is quite essential to intelligent reading or listening, for it enables us to do justice to the
arguments of others, to see their strength or to detect
their fallacies. To read profitably we must form
conclusions from the evidence furnished by the
author, and test his theories and conclusions by the
evidence we have gained from him or from others.

Mere acquisitiveness is not a scholarly trait; the scholar accepts the contributions of others as the data upon which to base his own judgments.

Not all of these reasoning processes would be, in the strictest sense, called argumentation, for argument proper postulates or assumes a proposition to be proved. Reaching the proposition or conclusion is, however, in many cases, the most vital part of the operation. Besides, all propositions are not equally suitable for argument, and we make sorry work of arguing if we start with a poor proposition. For these reasons we shall make it our business to find how a proposition for argument is obtained as well as how its truth or falsity is demonstrated. This preliminary work may be broadly classified under three heads, — Selecting the Question, Deciding on the Proposition, and Stating the Proposition.

FINDING THE PROPOSITION

SELECTING THE QUESTION

THE student who wishes to derive full benefit from the study of argumentation will do well to resist the temptation to consult published lists of questions for debate or to ask some friend to suggest an appropriate subject. The best question is one that grows out of one's own experience. We are living to little purpose if circumstances and events do not make us think, do not stimulate in us questions, and give rise to problems to which we wish to find the answers. One who has this habit of incurious acceptance of whatever comes to one without inquiry can not be too soon rid of it.

The man who is able to work out and test the solution of problems proposed by others is a serviceable man for routine work. But the one who takes the initiative, who suggests the problem, who proposes the solution, is indispensable to progress. Many surgeons stand ready to perform the operation when the master surgeon has diagnosed the case and inferred the source of the trouble from the symptoms; the schoolboy can test Newton's law of gravitation; Columbus had followers in plenty; steamboats, locomotives, cotton gins, sewing machines, were manufactured by the thousand after the first was made; a higher law than that of an eye for an eye and a tooth for a tooth having been uttered, ordinary men can preach it. The inventor, pointing the way to improved methods; the general, foreseeing the enemy's move; the prophet, announcing the need of social reform, — these rather than the mechanic at his bench, the man behind the gun, the faithful disciple, are the men we wish to emulate. The quality that makes them great is called for by the everyday affairs of life. In general, the head is more important than the hand; the housekeeper, not the servants, the merchant not the clerks, the teacher not the students, is held responsible for the failure or success of the home, the shop, the school.

Since, then, to project is important as well as to carry into effect, we must not let others do this valuable part of our work for us. It is not enough to prove a proposition derived by another; we should not be willing to surrender our right to the initiative to any one else. We must cultivate the habit of originating questions. Let us look into our own experience and see if questions for discussion do not suggest themselves. It is not supposable that they will be questions that have never been discussed. They may have been debated for hundreds of years and yet be original for us. If a personal experience has vitalized the question, has made it one that we have an actual interest in seeing answered, or one that we have worked out to our own satisfaction, it is sufficiently our question. It is not imposed from without, but springs from within.

Debatable questions may be argued, but a good question for argument is not necessarily debatable. If we sustain a proposition with evidence, we argue, whether or not there is anything to be said on the other side. That *Two Gentlemen of Verona* is one of Shakespeare's earlier plays is scarcely open to question, but to prove by evidence taken from the play itself the immaturity of the playwright would make an interesting argument. It adds to the zest for argument to take a question upon which there is difference of opinion.

The student is at liberty to select questions upon which he has made up his mind and concerning which he wants to win others to adopt his views, or questions about whose solution he is in doubt and regarding which he wishes to reach a conclusion for his own satisfaction. But he should be careful to select questions that do not call for too much research, questions in a field where he has a background of knowledge. A question may be genuine enough, the student may sincerely want to know the answer, but if the mystery is easily penetrated and due only to the peculiar ignorance of the questioner, the question is not a good one for argument. A child

may honestly wonder what makes the clock strike;
why his father prefers the pages of the Sunday paper
that have no pictures; why moisture forms on the
outside of a glass of water on a warm day; where the
sun goes when it sets; and get some good mental
training from his efforts to solve these questions, but
he does not advance much in his search for truth.
So a student may take a speculative question, and by
ingenious reasoning on false premises get beneficial
mental gymnastics; but except for the purpose of
humor it is not satisfying to put effort and time on
problems that a little investigation rightly directed
would solve.

A background of knowledge of the subject from
which the question is chosen is important not only
to prevent the student's deciding upon questions
based on easily penetrated difficulties, but also to
insure his deciding upon a question that can be
discussed in a sensible way without too much study.
One is ill at ease in an unfamiliar subject, aware that
he may make absurd mistakes where he least expects
to do so.   The pressure of other work is usually too
great to permit a student in a composition course to
add to the labor of selecting, arranging, and presenting his material the labor of finding it.

The question, then, should be one that interests the
writer, preferably one that is debatable, one that has to
do with subject-matter that is familiar to the inquirer.

EXERCISES

1. Tell why each one of the following questions would or would not be a suitable question for you to debate : —

a. Was Jefferson a greater statesman than Washington?

b. Is English literature greater than German literature?

c. What is the best method of increasing our national revenue?

d. Should I try to win one of the Cecil Rhodes scholarships?

e. Will flying machines ever come into general use?

f. Should the lives of writers be studied in literature classes?

g. Is a doctor's life harder than a farmer's?

h. Was Lady Macbeth more responsible than Macbeth for the murder of Duncan?

i. Should the book stacks in public libraries be open to the public?

j. Should the department method of teaching be introduced into the grammar grades of the public schools?

k. Is the earth spherical?

2. Read the facts and the opinions given below, and write a list of questions for discussion suggested by them : —

" The conscious use of the words or the ideas of another without giving credit to their author is called plagiarism.

"Students should remember that (1) whenever they give another's words exactly, quote him, they should place the words within quotation marks, and in a footnote acknowledge their indebtedness, naming the source of the quotation, giving the chapter or page, and, if there is more than one volume or edition, the volume and the edition used; (2) they should not by mere paraphrasing seek to win credit for ideas that are really another's." — G. P. BAKER : *The Principles of Argumentation*.

"Thus Mirabeau plagiarized every good thought, every good word, that was spoken in France. Dumont relates that he sat in the gallery of the Convention and heard Mirabeau make a speech. It struck Dumont that he could fit it with a peroration, which he wrote in pencil immediately and showed to Lord Elgin, who sat by him. Lord Elgin approved it, and Dumont, in the evening, showed it to Mirabeau. Mirabeau read it, pronounced it admirable, and declared he would incorporate it into his harangue, to-morrow, to the Assembly. 'It is impossible,' said Dumont, 'as, unfortunately, I have shown it to Lord Elgin.' 'If you have shown it to Lord Elgin, and to fifty persons besides, I shall still speak it to-morrow;' and he did speak it, with much effect, at the next day's session. For Mirabeau, with his overpowering personality, felt that these things, which his presence inspired, were as much his own, as if he had said them, and that his adoption of them gave them their weight." — EMERSON : *Napoleon*.

" . . . The charge of plagiarism is hardly ever made but by plagiarists, and persons of the unhappy class who do not believe in honesty but on evidence. . . . I have so often spoken, in the preceding pages, of Holman Hunt's picture of the 'Light of the World,' that I may as well, in this place, glance at the envious charge against it, of being plagiarized from a German print.

"It is indeed true that there was a painting of the subject before ; and there were, of course, no paintings of the Nativity before Raphael's time, nor of the Last Supper before Leonardo's, else those masters could have laid no claim to originality. But what was still more singular (the verse to be illustrated being, 'Behold, I stand at the door and knock'), the principal figure in the antecedent picture was knocking at a door, knocked with its right hand, and had its face turned to the spectator! Nay, it was even robed in a long robe, down to its feet. All these circumstances were the same in Mr. Hunt's picture; and as the chances evidently were a hundred to one that if he had not been helped to the ideas by the German artist, he would have represented the figure as *not* knocking at any door, as turning its back to the spectator, and as dressed in a short robe, the plagiarism was considered as demonstrated. Of course no defense is possible in such a case. All I can say is that I shall be sincerely grateful to any unconscientious persons who will adapt a few more German prints in the same manner.

"Finally, touching plagiarism in general, it is to be remembered that all men who have sense and feeling are being continually helped: they are taught by every person whom they meet, and enriched by everything that falls in their way. The greatest is he who has been oftenest aided; and if the attainments of all human minds could be traced to their real sources, it would be found that the world had been laid most under contribution by the men of most original power, and that every day of their existence deepened their debt to their race, while it enlarged their gifts to it. The labor devoted to trace the origin of any thought, or any invention, will usually issue in the blank conclusion that there is nothing new under the sun; yet nothing that is truly great can be altogether borrowed; and he is commonly the wisest, and is always the happiest, who receives simply, and without envious question, whatever good is offered him, with thanks to the immediate giver." — Ruskin: *Modern Painters.*

In many of our best schools and colleges students found guilty of plagiarism are expelled.

The purpose of a composition course in school or college is not to secure literary masterpieces; it is to train students to think and to express their thoughts correctly and effectively.

Shakespeare consciously used the words and the ideas of others in writing his plays.

"Facts are not copyrighted; but unless a writer is accepted as himself an authority, he is expected to tell where he found them. Form, that is order, grouping, is private property, copyrighted, not to be reproduced without paying royalty, not worth reproducing anyway, since the whole point of writing at all is thereby lost. Phrase is as strictly private as its maker's purse. It may, of course, be quoted, with citation as of fact; but frequent quotation is tiresome and unprofitable. Use without quotation is theft." — BALDWIN: *A College Manual of Rhetoric.*

Concerning Washington's *Farewell Address* Norman Hapgood writes that though written by Hamilton, "The credit is properly given to Washington by the world for the experience was his, the solution his, Hamilton his."

3. Write an argumentative dialogue between two students on one of the questions you have suggested.

4. Come to class prepared to take part in a general informal debate in which each member of the class will be allowed to speak on either side of the question: Is a student in this class justified in using the words or the ideas of another without giving credit to the one who originated them? In your speech you should state some reason for

thinking plagiarism justifiable or unjustifiable and give evidence that what you say is true.

5. If all the tickets to your Glee Club Concert had been sold and you were to see the following notice on the bulletin board, what questions should you feel inclined to ask?

Students are warned not to resell their Glee Club Concert tickets at advanced price. A severe penalty will be inflicted on all offenders. — BUSINESS MANAGER OF GLEE CLUB.

6. Look carefully through Hawthorne's *House of the Seven Gables* to discover whether or no the author had a definite plan of the house in his mind. Draw a ground plan of the house, and cite passages from the book that make you think the rooms were arranged as you have represented them.[1]

7. Suggest for discussion some change that would in your opinion benefit your school; your town; a text-book; some story you have read.

[1] This exercise was suggested to the writer by the discussion of the question in Mrs. H. A. Davidson's introduction to *The House of the Seven Gables.*

DECIDING ON THE PROPOSITION

HAVING selected a question both interesting and familiar, we must next reach a conclusion regarding this question that can be stated in a proposition which shall form the basis for argument.

It is possible to make others believe that a conclusion is true which you believe to be false. Lawyers doubtless often do this; a student in a debate course necessarily sometimes takes what seems to him the weaker side of the question. It is good discipline for a student to be obliged to see so clearly the strong points in the side of the case that does not enlist his sympathy that he is able successfully to advocate it. But in general argumentation it is not necessary, and for some reasons it seems unwise, to attempt to prove what one does not believe to be true.

In the first place, faith in your case makes your work lighter. If you are sure you are in the right, it seems worth while to exert yourself to make others see as you see, and you are willing to encounter difficulties to prove your point. If you have no convictions either way, or if you see the weakness of your own case, it is hard to work with ardor. Rufus

Choate said: "I care not how hard the case is. It may bristle with difficulties. If I feel that I am on the right side, that case I win."

It was so distasteful to Abraham Lincoln to make the worse appear the better reason that he made it a rule to advocate only the side that he believed to be right. The moral force he consequently threw into his argument made "Honest Abe" an opponent that few could match.

In the second place, argument for argument's sake leads to the habit of specious reasoning, of caring more to make an appearance of right, than to make right appear. If argument teaches us merely to confound our opponents with concealments, subterfuges, ridicule, and tricks, it falls far short of its right purpose. As students we should be open minded and interested, not in "making a case" as they say, but in discovering and making plain the truth, and a course in argumentation should teach us to do that. Too often the young orator and debater takes as an example for emulation the demagogue, the man who plays upon the ignorance and weakness and prejudice of his hearers and relies upon his skill in doing so to make his point. The would-be debater should look for models rather among the philosophers, the scientists, the statesmen, men who assume on the part of their readers and hearers an intelligence equal to their own; who would not stoop to trickery and devices to gain adherents, but offer only such reasons as seem to them convincing, and depend on the strength of their cause for success.

Since it is important to take the right side of an argument the student should not jump rashly to his conclusion.   He should decide on his proposition only after careful reasoning.

All reasoning is from the known to the unknown. From known particular instances we may infer an unknown general truth ; from a known general truth we may pronounce concerning an unknown particular case; we may reason from what is happening to the unknown that will happen or that has happened in the past.

When from particular cases that have come under our observation we infer general truths, we reason inductively.   The inductive method of reasoning is the laboratory method ; the scientist performs the experiment, makes his observations, and so accumulates the data upon which to base a generalization. But this method of reasoning is not used by the scientist alone.   Men, women, and children daily generalize from their experience.

A woman on moving from the country into the city, finding that Mrs. Stone, Mrs. Flint, and Mrs. Steel manifest no interest in her affairs, and remembering how Mrs. Hay, Mrs. Greene, and Mrs. Field listened with eagerness to her domestic experiences, may make the generalization that city people are less sympathetic than country people. Her line of reasoning is a safe one : what is true of the several members of a class is true of the class. The scientist observes that each woodpecker he examines has a strong chisel-like bill, rigid and acuminate tail feathers, toes arranged in pairs, etc., and concludes that all woodpeckers have these characteristics.   The countrywoman and the scientist both draw conclusions from the facts that have come within their observation.   But the generalization reached by the biologist is more trustworthy than that reached by the countrywoman.   The difference lies in the fact that he has observed an almost unlimited number of woodpeckers, while she has observed a limited number of country people and a limited number of city people.   He has observed exactly and has counted as common only those attributes that are characteristic of all.   She, on the other hand, has inaccurately attributed the broad term "sympathy" to her country friends because they have been ready to enter into her personal affairs; she has denied it to her city acquaintances because they treated it as a slight matter that her unexpected guest found the dinner table covered with a striped cloth rather than a spotted one, or that she had to wash her windows with unreasonable frequency, and so on.

It is quite possible that she should find country

people who could not share her interest in these matters, and city people who could. Moreover, her test is not a significant one. On closer acquaintance and tried by other measures Mrs. Steel might prove more truly sympathetic than Mrs. Field.

In inductive reasoning one should be careful to study a large number of facts on which to base his conclusions and should make no claim that the facts do not justify. After reading *The Snow Image*, *The Great Stone Face*, *Drowne's Wooden Image*, *Wakefield*, one might draw the conclusion that Hawthorne's stories are light and pleasing; while a reader of *The House of the Seven Gables*, *Ethan Brand*, and *The Scarlet Letter* might pronounce the same author's works morbid. It is possible, too, that other readers pronouncing on the same books might find the second group not morbid and the first not light.

Generalizations may be unreliable because they are supported by too few specific instances or because the supporting assertions are in themselves not true. I may assert that every person in the room has read *David Copperfield*, for Mary Smith has read it, James Moore has read it, Fred Harrison has read it, and Flora Mason has read it. And Thomas Wilson may remind me that he is present and that he has not read the book. Or Fred Harrison may say, "You are mistaken; I could talk with you about Mr. Micawber, Uriah Heep, Betsey Trotwood, and Peggotty because my father often quotes them, but I have never read *David Copperfield*." In either case my generalization is disproved.

There are various ways of becoming aware of an unknown specific truth. I may know an apple is sour because I have tasted it. I may know it through the experience of another; or I may infer that it is sour from certain observed facts. I may infer that it is sour because I know from what tree it was picked, and past experience has led me to believe that the tree in question bears only sour apples. I may infer that the apple is sour because it is small and green and hard, and past experience has taught me that apples having that appearance are sour. Or I may infer that the apple is sour from the fact that the boy eating it is puckering up his face just as I have done when I have tasted sour apples.

In making each of these inferences or deductions I have reached an unknown fact about a particular apple through familiarity with certain classes of apples and knowledge of the particular apple that enabled me to put it into the known class. I know concerning all apples that grow on a certain tree that they are sour. I know that this particular apple may be classed as the fruit of that tree. Then, since each member of a class must have the attributes of the class, this apple must have the attribute sourness that has been predicated of all the apples that grow on that tree.

My reasoning simply expressed is,

> All apples that grow on that tree are sour.
> This apple grew on that tree.
> This apple is sour.

If it is granted that all the eggs in the refrigerator are fresh, then those in the basket must be fresh, for the basket is in the refrigerator. If all the men on a ball team are known to be good players and I can show that any individual is a member of the team, I need no further argument to prove him a good player.

This combination of assertions, the predication of an attribute to a class, the assertion that a particular object or objects belong to that class, and the assertion that the particular object has the attribute ascribed to the class, is called a syllogism. The three propositions are called respectively the major premise, the minor premise, and the conclusion.

Major premise.— All members of the Symphony Orchestra are skilled musicians.

Minor premise. — Mr. Forbes is a member of the Symphony Orchestra.

Conclusion. — Mr. Forbes is a skilled musician.

In ordinary speech a syllogism is usually contracted into an enthymeme; that is, only two of the three propositions are expressed, as Mr. Forbes is a skilled musician, for he is a member of the Symphony Orchestra; or Mr. Forbes is a skilled musician, for all members of the Symphony Orchestra are skilled musicians; or Mr. Forbes is a member of the Symphony Orchestra, and all members of the Symphony Orchestra are skilled musicians.

It will be noticed that the third proposition may be readily inferred from the other two. Only three terms are possible in a syllogism, and any two propositions must contain all three of them, since the major premise has for its predicate the major term of the syllogism; the minor premise has for its subject the minor term of the syllogism; the conclusion has for its subject the minor term, for its predicate the major term; and the middle term occurs as the subject of the major premise and the predicate of the minor premise.

In the syllogism last considered *the members of the Symphony Orchestra* is the middle term; *skilled musicians* is the major term, and *Mr. Forbes* is the minor term. The middle term is the known class; the minor term, the partly known individual member of that class; the major term, the attribute that is known to belong to the class and hence to the individual member of the class.

It is clear that in order that the truth of the conclusion should inevitably follow from the premises the major premise must be universal; that is, every member of the class must be included. If there are any exceptions, if some members of the Orchestra are not skilled musicians, the fact that Mr. Forbes is a member of the Orchestra will not prove him a skilled musician. *All* is the sign of the universal affirmative proposition.

Other forms of syllogisms are possible, but confusion and difficulty will be avoided by following the form given. If the major premise is not an affirmative universal proposition, it should be made so. If we take the premises, No artist is indifferent to criticism, and Mr. Black is an artist, we can not take the predicate of the major premise unchanged as the predicate of the conclusion.

But the major premise may be obverted or changed to an affirmative statement without changing its meaning. No artist is indifferent to criticism, may be changed to, All artists are sensitive to criticism ; or it may be more accurately changed by using *all* where *no* was used in the subject and introducing the negative into the major term, as, All artists are men who are not indifferent to criticism. With either of these affirmative, universal propositions for a major premise a normal syllogism may easily be constructed : —

All artists are sensitive to criticism.
Mr. Black is an artist.
Mr. Black is sensitive to criticism ;
or,
All artists are men who are not indifferent to criticism.
Mr. Black is an artist.
Mr. Black is a man who is not indifferent to criticism.

In an enthymeme the universal proposition is often disguised so that it is a little hard to recognize it. The statement, If Mr. Adams said it, it must be true, is easily expanded into a regular syllogism: —

All that Mr. Adams says is true.
This is something that Mr. Adams said.
This is true.

Or, the statement that Mr. Davis is lucky, for a man must be either very clever or very lucky to play the game so successfully, implies the following syllogism:

All men who play the game so successfully and are not clever are lucky.
Mr. Davis is a man who plays the game successfully and is not clever.
Mr. Davis is lucky.

In syllogistic reasoning the premises must be true and the relation between them right or the conclusion is unreliable.

The proposition you decide upon for an argument should be a conclusion that rests on a granted major proposition and a provable minor proposition.

EXERCISES

1. Come to class prepared to take part in an informal, general debate on the question: Should students be required to support in debate the side that they do not believe to be right?[1]

[1] The most excellent drill in argument is afforded by general informal class-room discussions of questions upon which all are fitted,

2. What was the fault in the reasoning of the peas in the fairy tale, that looked about them and concluded the world was green?

3. Read the following fable; express in the form of a syllogism the donkey's reasoning, and tell why his conclusion was wrong.

A donkey laden with salt in crossing a stream stumbled and fell into the water. Before he regained his feet most of the salt had dissolved and his burden was much lighter. The next time he traveled that way he was carrying a load of sponge. Remembering his former experience he purposely fell and let his burden lie for some minutes in the water.

4. During the debate on the Mills Bill, a prominent Republican member of Congress replied to a speech made by Mr. Morse of Boston against the high tariff on wool and the consequent high price of clothing, by saying in substance : It is the old story of the man who gets a dollar a day for his wages, and having worked ten days goes to buy his suit of clothes. He expects to buy the suit for ten dol-

without special preparation, to express an opinion, and upon which there will naturally be some diversity of opinion. It is in such debates as these in real life, in the home, in the faculty meeting, in the committee room, the directors' meeting, that vital debate is done rather than in prepared speeches. While it is advisable for every student to come to class with a definite point to be proved and the evidence with which to prove it in mind, spontaneity should be cultivated. The quick and timely support or overthrow of a classmate's argument should be a student's aim quite as much as the offering of independent arguments. The prearranged speech has little value in training boys and girls to speak in comparison with the speech suggested by the remarks of another and made with reference to what has been said on the subject during the discussion.

lars. But the robber manufacturers have been to Congress and have got one hundred per cent put upon the goods in the shape of a tariff, and he must pay twenty dollars. So he must go back to ten days more of sweat, ten days more of toil, to earn the ten dollars needed to pay for the clothes. Here, said the congressman [unwrapping a parcel and holding up a suit of clothes], is the entire suit, tariff and all, for just ten dollars.

Tell what syllogism is implied by the enthymeme: This suit of clothes disproves the theory that the tariff on wool causes a man to pay $20 for a $10 suit of clothes, for this suit, tariff and all, cost $10. Which premise has been proved? Why, then, is the argument not convincing?

5. Tell what is wrong in the reasoning of the blind men in the following : —

"The First approached the Elephant,
       And happening to fall
   Against his broad and sturdy side,
       At once began to bawl :
   'God bless me ! — but the Elephant
       Is very like a wall.'

"The Second, feeling of the tusk,
       Cried, 'Ho ! what have we here
   So very round and smooth and sharp ?
       To me 'tis mighty clear
   This wonder of an Elephant
       Is very like a spear !'

"The Third approached the animal,
       And, happening to take
   The squirming trunk within his hands,

Thus boldly up and spake : —
' I see,' quoth he, ' the Elephant
Is very like a snake : '

"The Fourth reached out his eager hand,
    And felt about the knee ;
' What most this wondrous beast is like
    Is mighty plain,' quoth he ;
' 'Tis clear enough the Elephant
    Is very like a tree ! '

"The Fifth, who chanced to touch the ear,
    Said, ' E'en the blindest man
Can tell what this resembles most :
    Deny the fact who can,
This marvel of an Elephant
    Is very like a fan ! '

"The Sixth no sooner had begun
    About the beast to grope,
Than seizing on the swinging tail
    That fell within his scope,
' I see,' quoth he, ' the Elephant
    Is very like a rope ! ' "
    — SAXE : *The Blind Men and the Elephant.*

6. Read the following newspaper clipping and give the untenable major premise and the unprovable minor premise that are necessary to the conclusion, — " then we have an instance of telepathy between a dog and a human being."

LONDON, July 25.

" Much public attention has been attracted by a remarkable dream story sent to the press by H. Rider Haggard.

He says that on July 10 he suffered a painful nightmare, and while still half conscious dreamed that his favorite retriever was dying, that he himself was close to it and that the dog was endeavoring to tell him the facts. The body of the retriever was found in the river three days afterward, and an investigation seems to prove that it was killed on July 10 by a train about three hours before Haggard's dream.

" The only doubt about the facts, as to most of which Haggard produces full corroborative evidence, is as to the time, for, if the dog was killed later, the incident is reduced to a dream which turned out true, an experience by no means unusual. Mr. Haggard, however, has satisfied himself as to the manner and time of death and seems convinced that the dog did, either at the moment of death or after it, succeed in telling his master what happened. If the communication was made at the moment of death, then we have an instance of telepathy between a dog and a human being without precedent, while, if it was made after death, Mr. Haggard suggests that some non-bodily but surviving part of life or the spirit of the dog reproduced those things in his mind.

" The incident has already induced a flood of correspondence on the subject."

7. From the following terms construct syllogisms : —

Major term	Minor term	Middle term
brave	Richard	warriors
good students	Fred West	members of the football team
true	That Cæsar is ambitious	what Brutus says
interesting	*Praeterita*	autobiographies of great men

| *Major term* | *Minor term* | *Middle term* |
| stores that sell shoes | Wilson and Smith's store | department stores |

8. Express in the form of universal affirmative propositions : —

No college work is easy.

None but the brave deserve the fair.

Only just acts are kind.

He jests at scars who never felt a wound.

A man must be stupid or unkind who habitually hurts the feelings of others.

9. From the following enthymemes construct syllogisms : —

This orange is seedless, for it is a navel orange.

The tree you speak of is an apple tree, for all the trees in my father's orchard are apple trees.

She must be a good student, for only good students are given scholarships.

All men are fallible, and the king is a man.

10. From each of the syllogisms you have constructed derive the two enthymemes that have not been furnished.

STATING THE PROPOSITION

In clubs, debating societies, courts, legislative bodies, wherever formal arguing is done, it is customary to reduce the question in controversy to a statement. This is necessary since we seek by argument to prove the truth. As a word or phrase asserts nothing, it can not be true or false; the idea to be proved must therefore be expressed as a proposition.

Ordinarily a proposition to be debated is engrossed in a resolution, as: Resolved, That *immigration should be further restricted*. This statement may serve for an argument intended to prove either side of the question. The statement is affirmative, and the one arguing for further restriction of immigration would be taking the affirmative side of the argument. One arguing against further restriction would be taking the negative. Had the statement been negative, Resolved, That *immigration should not be further restricted*, the one who argued against further restriction would have the affirmative, and the one who argued for the restriction the negative.

The negative form of statement is sometimes preferable. This is the case when your argument is to be in the nature of a defense, for the privilege of opening the discussion lies with the affirmative. It would seem gratuitous to begin a defense of a man or a measure that had not been assailed. If it were your purpose to justify General Harrison's advance on Tippecanoe, you should not state the resolution, Resolved, That General Harrison's advance on Tippecanoe was justified, and take the affirmative, but rather give the proposition the negative form, Resolved, That General Harrison's advance on Tippecanoe was not justified, and take the negative. This implies that General Harrison's action has been called into question and that there is some occasion for your championing his cause.

The student should remember that the affirmative or negative proposition does not commit him to either side of the argument. One can not tell, by seeing the proposition alone, which side of the argument a writer or speaker intends to take. If a student intends to argue against a measure, the nature of the argument he intends to make will determine whether the proposition should be affirmative or negative. If his argument is to be positive in character, if he is going to advance reasons why immigration should not be further restricted, the proposition should be negative in form; if, on the other hand, his argument is to be negative in character, devoted to showing that the reasons advanced for the restriction are not adequate or sound, he does not dare to assume the burden of proof that falls on the affirmative, but must give the proposition the affirmative form and take the negative. It is a simpler matter to argue the negative of the proposition, immigration should be further restricted, than to take the affirmative of immigration should not be further restricted. Though both necessitate opposition to further restriction, the first task ends with proving further restriction not desirable, the second is completed only when further restriction has been proved actually undesirable.

Carelessness in phrasing the proposition is sure to lead one into difficulty in one way or another. Great care must be taken to make the proposition commensurate with the argument. That is, the statement should cover the entire argument and no more ; it should include the ultimate point to be argued and yet claim nothing that one does not intend to attempt to prove.

The student who stated his question thus, Resolved, That the United States government should build the Nicaragua Canal, when he wished not to argue that the undertaking should be assumed by the United States or that the Nicaragua route was preferable to the Panama, but simply that a transisthmian canal would be a great benefit to the world, signified too much in his proposition. His statement would demand for its proof the heaviest work on the points the student intended to ignore.

On the other hand, exactness demands that the proposition definitely express the limits of the question to be argued. The proposition, The college course should be shortened to three years, is, for example, too vague. The statement leaves one at sea as to whether the argument is intended to prove that the work now done in four years could be done in three; or that too much is attempted by the colleges, that their standards are too high, and that one year's work should be eliminated from the course; or that the entrance standards are too low; that the first year of college work properly belongs in the preparatory schools. It is evident that the statement of the proposition does not make clear the ultimate issue.

Carelessness as to the content of a proposition frequently results in a student's setting himself an absurdly easy or an absurdly difficult task. Prove any benefit, and you have proved that, The Salvation Army has done some good; you could scarcely prove that, No other organization could have accomplished so much good as the Salvation Army has accomplished.

Emphasis as well as content must be kept in mind in stating the proposition. A student whose main purpose was to prove that Mars must be inhabited by thinking creatures expressed his proposition thus, Resolved, That Mars is inhabited by beings superior

to human beings. As no word that is without significance is supposed to be admitted to the proposition,
this statement placing the emphasis on the relative
worth of the inhabitants of the two planets was misleading.

Further, the proposition must be clear. There
must be no uncertainty as to its meaning or the
meaning of its terms. Words should be used in their
accepted sense. A girl who wishes to argue that
geometry should not be required in the secondary
schools should not be satisfied with the phrasing,
Students should not be required to study mathematics.
The word "students" evidently needs modification.
Students in the elementary schools, students in advanced technical and scientific schools, she would not
intend to include in her argument, but so loose a
statement of the question necessitates their consideration. It is equally important that the relationship
between terms should be clear. Consider the proposition: Emerson is the most typical New England
writer. Does the student who presents this proposition wish to contend that Emerson is less eccentric
and has more traits in common with all New England
writers than has any other one New England writer,
or does he mean to show that Emerson more than
any other New England writer expresses the spirit
and genius of New England?

The wording of the question should be so impartial

and unprejudiced that it could serve as a basis for a negative or affirmative argument. The student who submitted the proposition, Resolved, That the impregnable fortifications at Port Arthur can not be taken by the Japanese, violated this canon. If we admit that the fortifications are impregnable, what is the use of arguing that they can or can not be taken? The word "impregnable" foredooms the argument to a single outcome.

Care should be taken to phrase the proposition in such a way as to insure unity of argument if possible. A compound proposition necessitates two nearly independent arguments. Domestic service is more beneficial than factory work, and Mary Blank should accept a position to do Mrs. Ball's housework rather than a position in a cotton factory, is a compound proposition and implies two virtually independent arguments, one on the 'general question, one on the specific question. As the purpose of the argument is to show what is best for Mary Blank, it is better not to consider the phases of the general question that do not pertain to her case, and to make the proposition entirely specific: Mary Blank should accept a position at Mrs. Ball's home, for general housework, rather than a situation in the village factory. The simple assertion permits a less divided structure than that suggested by the compound proposition.

EXERCISES

1. If you intended to prove that Thackeray was not a cynic, should you state the question in a negative or an affirmative proposition, and why ?

2. Criticise the following assertions as propositions for argument : —

a. Professor Wagner's method of teaching German is defensible.

b. The carrying of freight by rural electric cars is an industrial benefit, and a charter to carry freight ought to be granted to the company controlling the electric lines in Morgan County.

c. Slavish obedience to rules is not conducive to independence of character.

d. Travel will benefit a boy more than college.

e. The best way to uplift the Indian is to educate him.

f. Sensational newspaper articles do injury both to those about whom they are written and to those who read them, and they should be suppressed by law.

3. Comment on the difficulty of proving the following propositions, giving reasons for your judgment. Which proposition would, in your estimation, make the most satisfactory subject for an argument? Why?

a. American writers have been influenced by English writers.

b. All the works of American authors show the influence of some English author.

c. Washington Irving's works show the influence of certain English writers.

d. The influence of the *Sir Roger de Coverley Papers* on

Washington Irving's *Bracebridge Hall* is a good example of the influence of English writers on the early writers of the United States.

e. Washington Irving's *Bracebridge Hall* shows the influence of the *Sir Roger de Coverley Papers*.

4. What are the requirements of a good proposition for argument?

5. Bring to class a proposition on which you think you could write an argument of twenty pages.

PROVING THE PROPOSITION

ORGANIZATION OF MATERIAL — THE BRIEF

THE IMPORTANCE OF THE BRIEF

HAVING decided upon his proposition, the student's task is to prove it. If he has taken a familiar subject, his problem is to select and arrange the evidence at his command in the way best suited to prove his proposition. Whether he contemplates giving a written or an oral argument, a brief is indispensable at this stage of the work.

A brief is an outline or skeleton of an argument. It must be comprehensive enough to include the general plan of the argument. By the experienced brief-drawer the details of the plan may be presented with more or less elaborateness, but, because of the great value the brief has in training the student to organize his ideas, the brief of the beginner should be a full one.

Lincoln doubtless found the following brief adequate in a suit against an agent who had retained $200 out of $400 of pension money due the widow of a Revolutionary soldier : —

"No contract. — Not professional services. — Unreasonable charge. — Money retained by Def't not given to Pl'ff.

— Revolutionary War. — Describe Valley Forge privations. — Pl'ff's husband. — Soldier leaving home for army. — *Skin Def't.* — Close." — BAKER : *Principles of Argumentation.*

This brief, while sufficiently comprehensive, is too little elaborated to be helpful to an inexperienced writer. The following brief is a specimen of the kind of brief most helpful to the student : —

Question : Resolved, That the termite or white ant is an important agricultural agency in tropical Africa.

BRIEF FOR THE AFFIRMATIVE

INTRODUCTION

I. The extensive earth works of the termite, or white ant, suggest the question, May not this insect have an important agricultural function in tropical Africa ?

II. It is granted that earth loses its productive power unless the layers of soil are in some way mixed so that the subsoil is brought to the surface.

III. It is granted that any agency that is necessary to and largely instrumental in the bringing of the subsoil to the surface is an important agricultural influence.

IV. The question then is, Is the termite necessary to the bringing up of the subsoil in tropical Africa, and is it largely instrumental in the process ?

PROOF

The termite, or white ant, is an important agricultural agency in tropical Africa, for

I. It is necessary to the transference of the layers of soil, for

    A. Other agencies are wanting, for

        1. There are no frosts to disintegrate the soil.

    B. The work can not be done by the earthworm, for

        1. Although the earthworm is a "natural skewer,"

        1^1. Yet, it can not penetrate the sun-baked soil of the tropics in the dry season.

        2. Worms of all sorts are rare in the tropics even in wet weather, for

            a. Henry Drummond reports in *Tropical Africa*, page 130, that he never saw a single worm in Central Africa.

II. It is instrumental in bringing the subsoil to the surface, for

    A. Its habits of life demand it, for

        1. Its mode of building its house demands it, for

            a. It builds subterranean houses.

            b. It must bring up the excavated earth.

            c. It builds mounds.

            d. It must bring the material for them from under the earth, for

        (1) The termite never appears **above** ground, for

         (*a*) It is blind.

         (*b*) It has many enemies.

    2. Its mode of procuring its food demands it, for

      a. It builds long earthen tunnels while in quest of food, for

        (1) Its quest often leads it from the ground to the tree tops, for

         (*a*) Its food is dead wood.

        (2) It never comes above ground without shelter.

  B. The soil thus brought up is spread over the surface of the earth, for

    1. The tunnels and mounds are in time disintegrated by the tropical winds and rains.

    2. The streams help to distribute and deposit their dust.

III. It is *largely* instrumental in bringing up the subsoil, for

  A. It brings up great quantities of earth, for

    1. Its mounds are large, for

      a. The mounds of the white ant are often thirty or forty feet in diameter and from ten to fifteen feet in height.

    b. "The brick houses of the mission-
        aries near Lake Nyassa have all
        been built from a single ants' nest,
        and the quarry from which the ma-
        terial has been derived forms a pit
        beside the settlement some dozen
        feet in depth." — DRUMMOND.
    c. The ant-hills protect the hunters.
2. Its mounds are numerous, for
    a. "They look like cemeteries from a
        distance."
    b. "The smaller hills occur in myriads
        along the shores of Lake Tan-
        ganyika."
3. Its mounds extend over a large territory,
    for
    a. They are said to abound over the
        whole interior of Africa.
4. Its tunnels often nearly cover the trunks
    and branches of trees.
5. There are whole forests of trees covered
    with earthen tubes.

CONCLUSION

Since, then, the white ant in building its home and
sheltering tunnels brings to the surface an enormous
amount of subsoil that would be brought up in no
other way, and deposits it in such shape that it is

eventually distributed by wind and rain and streams over the surface of a large part of Central Africa, it may be said to be an important agricultural agency in that region.[1]

The untrained thinker finds it more difficult to make a brief or outline and use it than to write a paper without one. You remember that before David went out against Goliath he tried on the armor of Saul, but found that it cumbered him, and so went forth to slay the giant in his own way with his shepherd's sling. To the beginner the brief is as Saul's armor was to the boy David, a hindrance; he can do a better piece of work without it. But his object is not to do a specific piece of work well; it is to gain power to do future work well; and just as David had to learn to wear the armor of Saul and exchange the shepherd's method for the warrior's in order to lead the hosts of Israel to repeated victories, so the student must learn to make the scholar's method help rather than hinder him, if he is to do strong, effective work in the future.

By practice in brief-drawing one gains the power to plan work with certainty and facility; one comes to see ideas in their various possible relations and quickly to adjust them rightly and effectively. Readjustment is easily possible in the brief. To change

[1] The material for this brief is taken from Henry Drummond's *Tropical Africa*, Chapter VI.

the amplified, completed work without evidence of patching is difficult. The student who writes without a brief frequently presents work in which he himself perceives flaws in the organization of material, because the labor of alteration requires more time than he can give it. Whereas, had he by means of a brief carefully projected his work, he would have discovered the difficulty in time to remedy it with little effort or time.

When he has the unamplified, bare framework before him, the student can better judge of the actual strength of his argument than he can when the idea is garnished with fair words and persuasively presented in the finished work. He sees more justly where the evidence by which he would establish the truth of a proposition is strong and where it is weak.

THE INTRODUCTION TO THE BRIEF

MATERIAL AND IMMATERIAL ISSUES

In argument we take for granted an audience. It is best to assume a hearer or reader who holds views opposed to those we advocate, as, if we work with the possibility of hostile criticism in mind, we shall be more careful to build up an irrefragable argument than if we work believing that whatever we say will find easy acceptance. Some initial agreements are necessary before there can be any intelligent disagreement. Opponents must agree on the interpretation of the question — they must agree as to what point or points must be proved in order to prove the truth or the falsity of a proposition. This it is the business of the introduction to discover.

Usually there are within the general issue under discussion many particular or special issues. It is necessary to find out whether or no there are among these particular issues any that do not need argument, that both sides will admit as true. Any such are immaterial to the discussion. It is the chief function of the introduction to eliminate from the discussion immaterial issues and to discover the material issues.

Just what the material issues in a controversy are will depend upon circumstances. Let us take a very simple example : The proposition is, Miss Blank should have a coat made in x style. This may be resolved into two particular or special issues, Should Miss Blank have a new coat, and, if so, should it be made in x style ? Before we begin to argue we should know whether or not there is any disagreement as to the first of these particular issues. If both sides agree that she should have a new coat, it would obviously be a waste of time to argue that she should. That particular issue should be eliminated from the discussion, and the argument should be directed to the establishment or the overthrow of the second issue, The coat should be made in x style.

That in turn may be resolved into particular issues; as, Will a garment made in x style be æsthetically satisfactory? Will it be economically satisfactory? It is possible that both of these issues may call for debate. It is possible that either one may be eliminated as immaterial. Both sides might agree that x style was altogether satisfactory in so far as producing a pleasing appearance was concerned; or both sides might agree that the question of economy was not for Miss Blank a serious consideration. If the first issue were discarded, the only issue to be considered would be, Would a coat made in x style be economical for Miss Blank? if the second were rejected as immaterial, the remaining special issue would be, Would a coat made in x style be æsthetically satisfactory? On further analysis of either of these issues further agreement might be discovered. The question having been narrowed to the consideration of the æsthetic effect, that issue might disclose the two special issues, Would the garment in itself be beautiful, and would it be suitable for Miss Blank? and both might agree that the style in itself was good; that agreement would leave as the single material issue for discussion the question whether or not the style would be becoming to Miss Blank.

Again, let us suppose that Dr. A brings the charge that Mr. B owes him $50 for professional services. Mr. B may deny the charge, admitting that he did

not pay the money, but maintaining that the service
was not rendered. The point of difference then is,
Was the service rendered? Or Mr. B may admit that
the service was rendered and deny that the money
was not paid, offering as evidence a canceled bank
check for that amount paid to Dr. A on the date in
question. The point in disagreement then becomes,
Was the check in payment for this particular service?
Mr. B may admit the service, and admit that he has
not paid the bill, but claim that there was a previous
contract that there was to be no payment in case the
operation was not successful. The material issues,
then, are, Was there such a contract, and, if so, was
the operation successful?

We are not ready for argument until the question
has been analyzed to such an extent that we have
reached the point of difference, that is, until all
immaterial issues have been cast aside and the
particular issue or issues upon which the difference
of opinion rests, discovered.

It must be remembered that many issues that are
ruled out as immaterial to the discussion are immaterial only because both sides agree upon them. This
makes it important that one should not assume as
immaterial issues, issues that would not be conceded
as immaterial by one's opponents. The most elaborate
argument that x style will be becoming to Miss Blank
will count for nothing if your opponent attacks the

fundamental proposition, Miss Blank should have a
new coat, and shows that she should not have one
made in x style or any style.   On the other hand, it is
unwise to waste time and strength in proving what
your opponent will grant.   Your strength must be
centered on the material issues.

One who had served with Washington in the legis-
lature of Virginia and with Franklin in Congress
said : " I never heard either of them speak ten minutes at a time nor to any point but the main point,
which was to decide the question.   They laid their
shoulder to the great points, knowing that the little
ones would follow of themselves."

It was Lincoln's habit in court to begin by " giving
away his case," as it seemed to an unseasoned opponent, who with delight heard the older lawyer
grant to him one point after another until they came
to the material issues on which the question hinged.
There Lincoln focused his strength.   A case of this
sort, now famous, was his defense of the son of a
woman who had befriended him, against a charge
of murder.   He conceded to the opposing lawyers
many points that seemed to the spectators hope-
lessly to damage his client's case ; but the time when
the murder was claimed to have been committed and
in which it must have been committed if committed
by his client, the place where the deed was done,
and the position of the alleged eyewitness were points

that he emphasized. Further, he emphasized the witness's claim that the moon was shining brightly and the fact that without moonlight he could not have seen the act. The lawyer then took from his pocket an almanac and showed the judge and the jury that the moon was not shining at the time agreed upon for the murder.

One of the most disconcerting things that can happen to a debating team is to come before an audience prepared to make a strong argument for a particular issue, and find their opponents ready to grant them that issue and show that the question turns on another issue.

The success of the argument must depend largely upon the success of the introduction, upon the establishment of an acceptable basis of agreement as to just what must be proved to prove the proposition in question.

EXERCISES

1. In the following introductions to briefs what issues are eliminated from discussion as immaterial? What issues are recognized as material issues?

a. Resolved, That prisons should be made places for the reform instead of the punishment of criminals.

I. It is agreed, that

A. The entire penal system exists for the protection of society.

B. The state's duty to its law-abiding citizens is to be considered before its duty to lawbreakers.

II. The question then becomes, Can the state benefit the criminal without injury to society ?

b. Resolved, That the continuance of the George Junior Republic is justifiable.

I. All agree, that

A. The continuance of an institution may be justified by its aim, its methods, its results.

B. The aim of the George Junior Republic is good.

C. The results are not yet apparent.

II. The question then becomes, Are the methods of the George Junior Republic calculated to accomplish its aims?

2. Study the following resolutions and conditions, and from the material given construct introductions to briefs : —

a. Resolved, That Mary Jones shall go to college.

Mary Jones is the only daughter of a widow. Mary is an unusually capable, clear-headed, energetic girl about nineteen years old. She has graduated from the village high school with distinction and is ambitious to have a college education and make a career for herself. She is not selfish, however, but is devoted to her mother, and wants to do what will make her happy.

Mrs. Jones is about fifty-five years old. She has sufficient means to keep herself and her daughter comfortably. Mary is her pride and joy, and she thinks she would be supremely happy if Mary would stay at home and help her to enjoy the rest of her life, which she frequently says will not be long.

What is the wish of both ? What is the point of difference ?

b. Resolved, That it would be better for Sally Brown to do general housework in the home of Mrs. Morris than to accept a situation in a jewelry factory.

Sally Brown is a sensible, intelligent girl; she is an orphan, uneducated and without means of support. She has a good deal of self-respect and a strong desire for self-improvement. She has an opportunity to work in a large jewelry factory, where some four hundred young men and women are employed, for seven dollars a week. She can get a comfortable room and board for four dollars a week. She can also get a position to do general housework, at three dollars a week with good board and room, in the home of a college professor whose wife is a considerate, cultivated woman and has taken an interest in Sally. The girl has not had special training for either situation, but is confident that she could succeed in either.

c. Resolved, That *The Star* and *The Record* should consolidate.

The Record is an old, conservative paper with good standing, circulation, and advertising list, and an able editor. *The Star* is a new, progressive paper, without a reputation for reliability; its editorials are light, its advertising rate low. The capital invested in *The Record* is $20,000. The capital invested in *The Star* is $10,000. For years *The Record* has paid an average dividend of seven per cent on the money invested. *The Star* has not averaged more than one per cent. They are the only Republican papers in town. Some families take both papers, others take *The Star* or *The Record*. It has been proposed that the companies consolidate and publish but one paper.

(Considering the question as one of finance, the proprietors of one paper will favor the consolidation; the proprietors of the other will have to be convinced that the combination will be to their interest. Figures are given showing that the combination must result in a profit large enough to pay more than seven per cent on the combined capital of the two papers.   Give the issue exactly.)

THE TEST OF A GOOD INTRODUCTION TO A BRIEF

As has been shown, we may consider the proposition to be proved as the conclusion of a syllogism. The truth of the conclusion of a syllogism depends on the truth of the two premises that *logically* support it.   If they are both true, the conclusion must inevitably be true.   Together the premises form a sufficient reason for the truth of the conclusion.

Take the syllogism: —

All men who care more for the well-being of others than for their own comfort and pleasure are generous.

Mr. Hale is a man who cares more for the well-being of others than for his own comfort and pleasure.

Mr. Hale is generous.

How do we know that Mr. Hale is a generous man?   What is the test of generosity?   Mr. Hale is generous because any one who cares more for the well-being of others than for his own comfort and pleasure is generous, and Mr. Hale is a man who cares more for the well-being of others than for his own comfort and pleasure.   If the universal statement is admitted to be true, if caring more for the well-being of others than for one's own comfort and pleasure is the test of generosity, then, if Mr. Hale is proved to have this characteristic, he will be proved to be generous.

ARGUMENTATION — 5

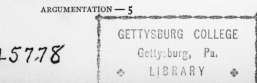

The introduction to a brief for an argument whose purpose was to prove the generosity of Mr. Hale might be something like this : —

I. Mr. Hale's refusal to contribute toward the building of the new library raises a question as to his generosity.

II. All agree, that

    A. A man may be generous without giving money to every worthy enterprise.

    B. All men who care more for the well-being of others than for their own comfort and pleasure are generous.

III. The question then resolves itself into this, Is Mr. Hale a man who cares more for the well-being of others than for his own comfort and pleasure?

It will be noticed that the material issue furnishes the middle term. As soon as we have reached that in the introduction to a brief we have the three terms for a syllogism, since we start with the conclusion in which the minor and the major terms occur. In the normal syllogism, it will have been noticed, the terms are arranged as follows : —

Major premise : middle term, major term.
Minor premise : minor term, middle term.
Conclusion : minor term, major term.

If the terms in the proposition or conclusion are not arranged in the right order, minor term, then major, it is necessary to put the conclusion into logical form before we can work back from it to the premises and complete the syllogism. If the proposition is, The negro should be given social recognition according to his individual merit, it is conceivable that different problems might be suggested by this proposition. From it the following syllogism might be evolved : —

Whatever is necessary to the negro's highest development is the negro's due.

Social recognition of the individual according to his merit is necessary to the negro's highest development.

Social recognition of the individual according to his merit is the negro's due.

Or,

All persons who deserve opportunity for the highest development should receive social recognition according to individual merit.

The negro is a person who deserves opportunity for the highest development.

The negro should receive social recognition according to his individual merit.

The minor and major terms in this proposition are rightly arranged for the conclusion of the first syllogism ; their order must be changed if the second syllogism is the one desired. Study of these syllogisms will show that, in each, the major premise of the one syllogism contains the idea of the minor premise of the other. If, then, both premises must be proved in order to prove the conclusion, it would be immaterial which syllogism were taken to epitomize the argument. But a comparison of the introduction and the syllogism given at the beginning of this chapter will show that the major premise expresses something agreed upon by both sides, and that the minor proposition expresses the point or points that must be proved by evidence. If, then, the first of the two syllogisms just given is taken, the argument will be limited to proving that the negro is a person deserving opportunity for the highest development. If the second is taken, the question for argument is simply, whether or not social recognition of the negro according to individual merit is essential to the highest development of the negro.

If the writer wishes to consider both questions in his argument, he will reject both of these limited syllogisms and take a more comprehensive one : —

Whatever is essential to the negro's highest development and whatever the white man owes the negro, should be given without consideration of the result to the white man.

Social recognition according to individual merit is something essential to the negro's highest development and something the white man owes the negro.

Social recognition of the negro according to individual merit is something that should be given the negro without consideration of the result to the white man.

The major premise thus often expresses a belief that may be regarded by some as debatable, but always one that must be accepted as unquestionable by those arguing from it. If the major premise, which corresponds to the fundamental agreements determined upon by the introduction and eliminated from the contention, is successfully assailed, no matter how firmly one establishes the minor premise, the conclusion is not proved.

After finishing his introduction the student should formulate his argument as a syllogism. If the introduction has discovered the middle term for this syllogism, established the major premise, and expressed the minor premise, it has prepared the way for the argument and is a good introduction. It is the business of the introduction to discover the middle term and establish the major premise. It is the business of the argument proper to prove by evidence that the minor premise is true or false.

EXERCISES

1. Write syllogisms using the material furnished by the introductions to briefs given in the first of the exercises beginning on page 62.

2. Write syllogisms testing the introductions you wrote from the material for introductions furnished on pages 63 and 64.

3. Write syllogisms using the material furnished by the following introductions : —

a Resolved, That football is a brutal sport.

I. All agree, that

> *A.* All games that depend for success on physical strength rather than on skill are brutal.

II. The question is, Does success in football depend on physical force rather than skill?

b. Resolved, That the present method of celebrating the Fourth of July should be changed.

I. All agree, that

> *A.* The Fourth of July is celebrated in order to foster patriotism and loyalty to government.
>
> *B.* The purpose of government is to protect the personal and property rights of the individual.

II. The question then becomes, Does the present method of celebrating the Fourth of July foster respect for the protection of the personal and property rights of the individual?

4. From the following propositions find the middle term for a possible syllogism and write out an introduction and a syllogism suggested by each.   (For suggestions as to how to obtain a universal affirmative major premise see page 34.)

Athletic contests between schools should be encouraged.

Fraternities should not be permitted in *x* schools.

Mr. N—— should locate his glass factory at —— (student may supply name of place).

Old Mr. and Mrs. Jackson should not sell their farm and move to the city.

Sam Bright should not leave school to take a clerkship in his father's store.

Public art galleries should be open on Sunday.

Dr. Mason should sell his horses and buy an automobile.

5. Read carefully the following introductions to speeches and from them write introductions to briefs : —

A. "Mr. President and Gentlemen of the Convention : If we could first know where we are, and whither we are tending, we could better judge what to do and how to do it. We are now far into the fifth year since a policy was initiated with the avowed object and confident promise of putting an end to slavery agitation. Under the operation of that policy, that agitation has not only not ceased, but has constantly augmented. In my opinion, it will not cease until a crisis shall have been reached and passed. 'A house divided against itself can not stand.' I believe this government can not endure permanently half slave and half free. I do not expect the Union to be dissolved — I do not expect the house to fall — but I do expect it will cease to be divided. It will become all one thing, or all the other. Either the opponents of slavery will arrest the further spread of it, and place it where the public mind shall rest in the belief that it is in the course of ultimate extinction ; or its advocates will push it forward till it shall become alike lawful in all the States, old as well as new, North as well as South. Have we no tendency to the latter condition? " — LINCOLN : *Springfield Address.*

B. " . . . In his speech last autumn at Columbus, Ohio, as reported in the *New York Times*, Senator Douglas said : —

" ' Our fathers when they framed the government under which we live, understood this question just as well, and even better, than we do now.'

" I fully indorse this, and I adopt it as a text for this discourse. I shall adopt it because it furnishes a precise and agreed starting point for a discussion between Republicans and that wing of the Democracy headed by Senator Douglas. It simply leaves the inquiry : What was the understanding those fathers had of the question mentioned?

"What is the frame of government under which we live? The answer must be, 'The Constitution of the United States.' That Constitution consists of the original, framed in 1787, and under which the present government first went into operation, and twelve subsequently framed amendments, the first ten of which were framed in 1789.

"Who were our fathers that framed the Constitution? I suppose the 'thirty-nine' who signed the original instrument may be fairly called our fathers who framed that part of the present government. It is almost exactly true to say they framed it, and it is altogether true to say they fairly represented the opinion and sentiment of the whole nation at that time. Their names being familiar to nearly all, and accessible to quite all, need not now be repeated.

"I take these thirty-nine, for the present, as being 'our fathers who framed the government under which we live.' What is the question which, according to the text, those fathers understood 'just as well, and even better, than we do now'?

"It is this: Does the proper division of local from Federal authority, or anything in the Constitution, forbid our Federal Government to control as to slavery in our Federal Territories?

"Upon this, Senator Douglas holds the affirmative, and Republicans the negative. This affirmation and denial form an issue; and this issue — this question — is precisely what the text declares our fathers understood 'better than we.' Let us now inquire whether the 'thirty-nine' or any of them ever acted upon this question; and if they did, how they acted upon it — how they expressed that better understanding." — LINCOLN : *Address at Cooper Institute.*

C. . . . "What I feared was, not the opposition of those who are averse to all reform, but the disunion of reformers.

I knew that, during three months, every reformer had been employed in conjecturing what the plan of the Government would be. I knew that every reformer had imagined in his own mind a scheme differing, doubtless, in some points from that which my noble friend, the Paymaster of the Forces, has developed. I felt, therefore, great apprehension that one person would be dissatisfied with one part of the bill, that another person would be dissatisfied with another part, and that thus our whole strength would be wasted in internal dissensions. That apprehension is now at an end. I have seen with delight the perfect concord which prevails among all who deserve the name of reformers in this House; and I trust that I may consider it as an omen of the concord which will prevail among reformers throughout the country. I will not, sir, at present express any opinion as to the details of the bill; but, having during the last twenty-four hours given the most diligent consideration to its general principles, I have no hesitation in pronouncing it a wise, noble, and comprehensive measure, skillfully framed for the healing of great distempers, for the securing at once of the public liberties and of the public repose, and for the reconciling and knitting together of all the orders of the State.

" The honorable baronet who has just sat down has told us that the ministers have attempted to unite two inconsistent principles in one abortive measure. Those were his very words. He thinks, if I understand him rightly, that we ought either to leave the representative system such as it is, or to make it perfectly symmetrical. I think, sir, that the ministers would have acted unwisely if they had taken either course. Their principle is plain, rational, and consistent. It is this, to admit the middle class to a large and direct share in the representation, without any violent shock to the institutions

of our country. . . .   I praise the ministers for not attempting, at the present time, to make the representation uniform.
I praise them for not effacing the old distinction between the
towns and the counties, and for not assigning members to
districts, according to the American practice, by the Rule
of Three.   The Government has, in my opinion, done all
that was necessary for the removal of a great practical evil
and no more than was necessary." — MACAULAY : *On the
Reform Bill;* House of Commons, March 2, 1831.

ADDED REQUIREMENTS FOR A GOOD INTRODUCTION

Very often the nature of the question under discussion makes the narrowing of the question to the
material issues a somewhat more complicated proceeding than it has thus far appeared.   Additional
steps are found to be helpful.

A clear statement of the occasion for the contention
or the cause of the difference of opinion frequently
helps to an understanding of just what the points at
issue are.   If the question is, Resolved, That I should
subscribe for the *Ladies' Home Journal* instead of
the *Atlantic Monthly* for Mary Blank next year, such
an introductory sentence, as, " The fact that the
leaves in Mary Blank's *Atlantic* are never cut makes
me wonder whether it is worth while to renew her
subscription next year," shows at once that the
argument is not concerned with the absolute excellence of either periodical, but with the suitability of
each to Mary Blank.

The following sentences in like manner indicate the trend of the argument to come : —

My income having been reduced one third by the failure of the *People's Bank*, I have been considering giving up my city home and taking a house in the suburbs.

The devastating forest fires we have had recently, again bring up the question, Is reasonable effort made to enforce the laws protecting the forests of this state?

The frequent assertion of college graduates that they learned more from their fellow-students while in college than from their professors does not seem to me so much to imply that they have learned little from their professors as that they have learned much from their classmates, and makes me wonder if the tutorial system is so desirable as the class method of instruction.

It is sometimes the case that, in spite of the utmost care in stating the proposition, terms are used that demand explanation. Take, for example, the question, Resolved, That the continuance of *The George Junior Republic* is justifiable. For the average audience, the term *The George Junior Republic* would require a brief explanation which should include for such an introduction as that given on page 63 a specific statement of the aims of *The George Junior Republic*. The definition of the term "justifiable" is directly involved in the narrowing of the question and ought by this time to be clearly understood. Still, it may be well to add a word of warning regarding a definition which must serve as a middle term in the syllogism, must furnish the criterion by which to judge. In such definitions synonyms must be avoided. Synonyms do help to make clear the meaning of unfamiliar words. But they do not help in the least to bring us nearer to argument. The student who says, "*Justifiable* will be used in this argument to mean defensible, warrantable," is no better off than before he said it. We are as much in need of a test of what is *defensible, warrantable* as we were of what was *justifiable*. If, however, he says, "An act may be said to be *justifiable* when its results show it to have benefited those affected by it," he has given us a gauge by which to measure the justifiability of an institution's continuance.

While an introduction to a brief may with perfect propriety contain, in addition to the statement of what issues are immaterial and what issues are material to the discussion, the statement of the origin of the question and an explanation of terms, care must be taken not to burden the introduction with unnecessary explanation. Such explanations as are essential should be given with as much brevity as is consonant with clearness. The definition of perfectly perspicuous terms is one form of unnecessary explanation. Akin to this fault of giving unneeded definitions is the one just considered, that of giving definitions that do not accomplish anything, the defining by synonyms.

But the most serious danger of overloading the

introduction lies in the statement of the material and the immaterial issues. Most students wish to tell why each point agreed upon is granted, or, in other words, to give the line of argument by which the opponents reached the agreement from which they start—to go back of the beginning. To do that is to fill the introduction with antecedent material no more relevant to the argument in hand than is the speed of the racers on their way to the race course to those who wait to see the race itself. There should be no argument in the introduction. What is given there is granted by both sides. It frequently happens that in great speeches there is just such argument in the introduction as students have been warned here not to use. This exists, however, as a conscious digression from the argument in hand, made because the speaker realizes that his audience, through forgetfulness or ignorance, is without the antecedent material necessary for intelligent acceptance of the basis of the argument. But all this is, for the person prepared to listen to the argument, as dispensable as would be a recital of the rules of the game at a football contest.

Restrictions of this sort are made for the purpose of strengthening the argument, and if a case occurs where the argument would be weaker for observing the rule, the rule should be sacrificed, not the argument. If the student, after careful consideration, feels that a few words of explanation would make clear an agreement that would be otherwise questioned, he should, of course, give them. It is best in such cases to summarize the reasons briefly and then give the conclusions, as : —

The inconvenience and delay to those who transact business there and the frequent accidents, make it plain that something must be done to relieve the congestion on Washington Street.

The impossibility of diverting traffic from Washington Street and the impracticability of widening the street convince all that relief must be sought by an overhead or underground railroad system, etc.[1]

So succinct a résumé of the grounds for agreement is not objectionable, if they are not perfectly obvious, but an elaborate presentation of evidence is out of place in the introduction. If the issues need argument, they are material issues and should be admitted to the argument proper.

Full statements rather than phrases should always be given in the introduction to the brief as well as in the brief proper. The phrase is unsatisfactory; it does not tell enough. Compare the following introductions : —

A

I. The origin of the question : —
   A. September entrance examinations.

[1] Suggested by Brief V in Baker's *Principles of Argumentation.*

II. Definition of terms : —
  A. Henry Mason.
  B. Mr. Linn's camp.

III. Immaterial issues : —
  A. Henry's object.
  B. Excellent tutors at his father's summer home.
  C. Standing of Mr. Linn's Camp.
  D. Henry's previous failures to remove conditions.
  E. Previous failures due to want of steady work.

IV. Material issue : —
  A. Place most conducive to steady work.

B

I. The origin of the question : —
  A. The fact that Henry Mason has to take the college entrance examinations in September, has brought up the question, Would it be advisable for him to spend his summer vacation in Mr. Linn's camp for boys?

II. Definition of terms : —
  A. Henry Mason is already twenty years of age; he lives in Boston and has had good educational opportunities, but he is not inclined to be studious.

B. Mr. Linn's camp for boys is a well-organized out-of-doors school in the White Mountains that has been established for the purpose of fitting boys to pass college entrance examinations.

III. Immaterial issues : —

A. Henry Mason and his parents agree that Henry's summer should be spent in the way best suited to insure his passing the examinations.

B. Good Harvard tutors can be had at Mr. Mason's summer home.

C. Mr. Linn's camp has been highly successful.

D. Henry has several times failed to pass off conditions in secondary school work which he has studied during the summer at his father's home.

E. These failures were due not to stupidity, but to want of steady application to study.

IV. Material issue : —

A. While Mr. Mason holds that a private tutor would be better for his son than a school made up of boys who probably care more for fun than books, Henry contends that the conditions at the camp are more favorable to steady work than those at his father's summer cottage.

Until one has read B, A seems quite blind and

unintelligible. The student's brief must be intelligible to others as well as to himself.

EXERCISES

1. Supply a suitable origin of the question for each of the introductions to briefs given in the Exercises on pages 62, 63, 69, 70.

2. Criticise the following introductions to briefs, and re-write : —

a. Resolved, That the regular school holiday should be changed from Saturday to Monday.

  I. Origin of the question : —

    A. The pupils' habit of coming to class Monday with unprepared lessons has given rise to the question, Should the regular school holiday be changed from Saturday to Monday?

  II. Definition of terms : —

    A. *The regular school holiday* is the day in each week on which, in addition to Sunday, children are excused from attending school.

    B. *Saturday* is the seventh day in the week.

    C. *Monday* is the second day in the week.

  III. Immaterial issues : It is agreed, that

    A. If the change were made there would not be, on the day after the weekly recess, so many students unprepared for class work, for

      1. The experiment has been made and has proved a success in this particular, for

        a. It was tried in x and the work of the students on Tuesday morning was much better than Monday morning work had been.

    b. In *y* the work was said to be better pre-
    pared for Tuesday morning than for any
    morning in the week.

    c. In *z* high school the principal reported the
    change was almost equivalent to a day added
    to the schedule.

   2. It is natural that it should be better, for

    a. Children frequently are not allowed to study
    on Sunday.

    b. Children forget before Monday what they
    have studied Friday evening or Saturday.

    c. Children are tempted to put off the prepa-
    ration of a lesson which they do not have to
    recite till the day after to-morrow.

    d. There is not so much going on on Monday
    to divert children from their study.

  B. The chief purpose of the weekly holiday is recreation, for

   1. Rest and pleasure have been found essential
   to the right development of children.

   2. Work suffers unless a child has sufficient recreation.

IV. Material issue : The question, then, is,

  A. Would the proposed change seriously interfere
  with the recreation of the pupils?

 b. Resolved, That Ernest Thompson Seton's animal
stories cultivate in boys the right attitude towards animals.

 I. Origin of the question :—

  A. My nephews' interest in the animal stories of
  Ernest Thompson Seton.

 II. Definition of terms : —

    A. Boys — between nine and fifteen.

    B. Right attitude — based on right understanding of animals.

III. Admitted facts : —

    A. Purpose of author to rouse reader's interest in animals and sympathy for them.

    B. Reader's interest in story aroused.

    C. Reader's sympathy for hero of story aroused.

IV. Debatable issues : —

    A. Writer's method conducive to cultivation of right understanding of actual animals?

c. Resolved, That modern illustrative methods have not contributed largely to real education.

I. Origin of the question : —

    A. The saying that our modern cheap illustrative process has provided a "royal road" to learning has raised the question, Has the omnipresent picture contributed to real education?

II. Definition of terms : —

    A. By *real education* is meant genuine cultivation.

III. Immaterial issues : —

    A. The question is not, Are pictures better and more numerous?

    B. The question is not, Have not pictures made it possible to see and understand much that we could not now understand without great effort without them?

IV. Material issues : —

    A. The question is, Has not the omnipresent picture educated the eye at the expense of the other senses?

B. Has it not made the mind too dependent upon
the eye for its images?

C. Does it not stultify rather than stimulate intellectual activity ?

3. Look over the addresses of distinguished orators till
you find an introduction that seems to you strong and complete.   Make a brief of it and bring it to class.

4. Bring to class an introduction for a brief on the question already submitted to instructor.   (See page 48.)

THE PROOF

The Classification of Evidence

The business of the brief proper is to build up an
irrefragable argument, to prove all that remains to
be proved after the introduction is completed.   The
introduction is important to the argument, since it
establishes the major premise on which the truth of
the conclusion partly rests.   But that premise is established by consent and not by argument.   The introduction finished, the making apparent the truth of
the proposition depends entirely on the proof of the
minor premise, which must be proved by argument.

If the question is in a field in which the writer is
not thoroughly informed, research for the purpose of
amassing evidence is a necessary preliminary to drawing up a brief ; but if the student is working, as at
this stage he should be, with familiar material and
has at hand most of the evidence he will need, he

may proceed, without reference to the chapter on research, to organize his evidence into a brief.

One may have at command a mass of evidence, direct and indirect, by which to prove a proposition, and yet not succeed in making a convincing argument. The evidence must be sifted and organized into a unified, coherent structure before it becomes effective. As a mob in which there is excellent material for an army, is comparatively ineffective because in it the potential brigadier is not distinguished from the major, the major from the captain, the captain from the private; just so an amorphous mass of evidence has little force because what ought to be leading propositions and what ought to be subordinate propositions are confused as equals.

The first task of organization is to sort the evidence and arrange it according to its rank or dependence. The introduction has given us a start here. The general proposition derived from the resolution under discussion is, as it were, commander in chief; those issues designated in the introduction as material issues give the propositions that are its immediate subordinates; they in turn are supported by other propositions, which must often themselves be supported; and so on.

One of the most frequent and serious faults of those inexperienced in drawing briefs is the failure to distinguish between coördinate and subordinate propositions. The beginner jots down as coördinate propositions, all the reasons, near and remote, for believing a proposition to be true that occur to him, and does not see that some of these are dependent on others.

Take, for example, the proposition, Corporal punishment is an objectionable mode of punishing children. Reasons for the truth of this proposition may present themselves to the mind helter-skelter : —

A. Corporal punishment causes physical injury and unnecessary suffering.

B. Whipping rouses resentment.

C. Severe corporal punishment is often followed by hours or days of languor and sickness.

D. Blows received from angry disciplinarians often result in permanent injuries.

E. Children's conduct is often worse after whipping than before.

F. Children taken from a disciplinarian who whips and placed under one whose methods are different have shown marked improvement.

G. Whipping does not help the child to distinguish between right and wrong.

H. Corporal punishment does not accomplish its purpose.

I. It does not develop character.

J. Corporal punishment makes the culprit keep

from wrongdoing for fear of pain rather than from a desire to do what is right.

K. Children have been made lame by corporal punishment.

L. Children have been made deaf by corporal punishment.

M. Corporal punishment makes children cowardly.

N. Corporal punishment makes children tell falsehoods to avoid pain.

The introduction to the brief will help to bring order out of this chaos. It might be as follows: —

I. Definition of terms: —

    A. Corporal punishment as used here includes slapping, whipping, or striking.

II. Immaterial issues: All agree, that

    A. The purpose of punishing children is to make them better.

    B. Punishment should not be of such a nature as to injure the child physically or give unnecessary pain.

    C. Any form of punishment that inflicts physical pain and injury and is morally ineffective is an objectionable form of punishment.

III. Material issues: The question is,

    A. Is corporal punishment, as here defined, physically injurious and morally ineffective?

The two propositions that include all ideas that come under the chief proposition are evidently: —

I. Corporal punishment is physically injurious.

II. Corporal punishment is morally ineffective.

If we look over the propositions we have made, we find that I means about the same as *A* and that it includes under it *C*, *D*, *K*, and *L*. We find that II expresses the idea expressed by propositions *H* and *I*, and that the remaining propositions are all in some way subordinate to it.

Returning to I and examining *C*, *D*, *K*, and *L*, we find that they are not coördinate. *C* seems more coördinate with *K* and *L* than with *D*, but does not belong under *D*. It is easy to supply a proposition that is coördinate with *D* of which *C* will be proof. The first section of the brief will then be as follows:

Corporal punishment is an objectionable mode of punishment for children, for

I. It is physically injurious, for

    A. Its temporary effects are often evil, for

      1. Children have been made sick and disabled by severe whipping and consequent crying.

    B. Its permanent effects are often evil, for

      1. Children have been made lame by corporal punishment.[1]

      2. Children have been made deaf by corporal punishment.[1]

[1] In a complete brief, specific cases should be cited to support this proposition.

There are more propositions to be grouped under II, and their arrangement will be more difficult. We find, however, after a little thought that three general propositions will cover all the propositions given : —

II. Corporal punishment is morally ineffective, for

>   *A.* It does not help the child to know the right.
>   *B.* It does not help the child to desire to do rightly.
>   *C.* It does not help the child to do rightly.

By a process similar to that already suggested, the propositions belonging under *A*, *B*, and *C* may be selected and supplied.

II. It is morally ineffective, for

>   *A.* It does not help the child to know what is right, for
>   >   1. It does not make evident the relation between the offence and the punishment.
>   >   2. It gives the child the idea that the physically weak must submit to the physically strong.
>   *B.* It does not help the child to desire to do rightly, for
>   >   1. It does not lead him to repent of his wrongdoing, for
>   >   >   *a.* It makes him more conscious of being wronged than of having done wrong.

      b. It leads him to wish to avoid pain rather than to wish to do what is right.

  2. It leads him to wish to do wrong, for

      a. It destroys his love and respect for those in authority over him.

      b. It makes many children sullen and resentful.

C. It does not help the child to do rightly, for

  1. It does not prevent the repetition of the same offence, for

      a. Children often repeat in defiance the offence for which they have been punished.

      b. Children become brutalized and deliberately commit an offence for which they know the penalty will be a whipping.

  2. It does not prevent the child's offending in other ways, for

      a. It leads him to lie to avoid pain.

      b. It leads him to concealment.

      c. It leads him to acts of vengeance.

Only complete simple propositions are used in the brief. All propositions in the brief are directly or indirectly related to the leading proposition ; the relationship is one that can be signified by the conjunction "for." The order throughout is, conclusion, then evidence. To get this firmly fixed in mind at the start will save the student much perplexity. It is really the order to which we are all accustomed. The teacher in the class room calls for your conclusion, then your evidence : you must tell what case a Latin noun is in and then give the reason that has led to your conclusion ; you must name the chemical compound and then tell the signs ; give the answer to the problem, then explain your process.

If you find yourself using in your brief such conjunctions as "as," "since," "hence," "therefore," "consequently," you may know immediately that your order is wrong, that you are giving the conclusion after the evidence rather than before it. " For " is a safe conjunction to use.

The requirement, conclusion before evidence, is one made not merely for uniformity, but because this order is more convincing. If you furnish your hearer or reader with the conclusion at the start, he knows just what is demanded of the evidence presented to him, and can as he receives it judge its adequacy. Whereas, if the evidence is presented first, the reader or hearer is not aware of what it is expected to prove and flounders blindly about in the dark, trying to find out for himself its purpose. When he reaches the conclusion, its statement either seems superfluous because he has already discovered it for himself, or, if he has not been able to infer it from the evidence, it seems questionable and he must review the points made to see if the conclusion is fully sustained. For the economy of mental effort, the order, conclusion before evidence, should be uniformly followed throughout the entire argument.

But, one might ask, is not the end the place for the conclusion. It is. It would be unfortunate to close a long argument with a bit of evidence for the truth of a conclusion almost lost sight of. It is, therefore, customary to append to the argument proper what is technically called the "conclusion." This is a short paragraph summing up the main lines of argument and stating the conclusion. In this final paragraph the order is reversed and the evidence is given first. The conjunctions used are, accordingly, those not used in the argument proper, "since," "as," "therefore." The paragraph ends with the statement of the proposition that has been proved.

For the convenience of the instructor in marking the papers there should be uniformity as to the symbols used to designate the rank and number of a proposition. Various methods are in use but the following is recommended: —

The main proposition, standing alone at the head of the argument without the possibility of a coördinate proposition, should not be numbered. The propositions that immediately support this proposition should be marked by Roman numerals. The propositions sustaining these propositions should be marked by capital letters; their subalterns by Arabic numerals, and so on : —

I.

   A.

      1.

      2.

         a.

            (1)

            (2)

            (3)

               (*a*)

  B.

      1.

         a.

         b. etc.

      2.

Each proposition after the main proposition should have before it one number or letter and only one. If a student finds himself writing *B* 1 before a proposition he may know that he has failed to insert a general proposition coördinate with the proposition marked *A*.

Only propositions bearing the relationship of reason or evidence to the proposition controlling them, should be lettered as subordinate to it. The relationship between proposition I and *A*, between *A* and 1, between 1 and *a*, etc., must be such that it can be expressed by the conjunction "for."

Coördinate propositions, all those designated by Roman numerals, all lettered by capitals, etc., must bear such a relationship to each other as could be expressed by " and " or " yet." The student should be sure that II and III, as well as I, are directly related to the main proposition as proof; *C, D, E*, as well as *A* and *B*, must be directly related as proof to I, II, or III. Every proposition in the brief proper must bear the relation of evidence to the one next above it in rank. A large number of coördinate propositions is usually a sign that the student has not examined his evidence closely enough to discover the existing relations of dependence.

In looking over a brief it is always well to glance at all the coördinate propositions of one rank before looking at the elaboration of any one. You should look at all propositions designated by Roman numerals before looking at *A, B*, and *C*, under any one of them. You should glance at *A, B*, and *C* under I before you look at 1, 2, 3, under *A*, and so on. Grasp the idea extensively; get the purpose and compass of the argument before you test a part of it intensively. This does not mean that you must partly work out the development of the argument under II and III before you complete the argument under I. After you have discovered II, III, IV, etc., you may leave them entirely until you have completed your analysis of I. After you have discovered *A, B, C, D*, etc., under I, you may leave *B, C*, and *D*, and focus your attention on *A*. When you have discovered 1, 2, 3, 4, etc., you may leave 2, 3, and 4, and give your attention to the proof of 1. The point is that you must recognize 2, 3, and 4 before you proceed to the development of 1. This is important not only in reading briefs; it is important also in drawing briefs, whether you are reducing a written argument to a brief, or are writing a brief to be developed into a forensic. The regular working order for analysis is : —

General proposition.
 I.
 II.
 III. etc.
—————
  I.
   A.
   B.
   C. etc.
   —————
    I. *A.*
     1.
     2.
     3. etc.
     —————
      I. *A.* 1.
       a.
       b.
       c. etc.
       —————

This, however, is not the order in which work is to be presented when finished.

EXERCISES

1. Supply a main proposition and subproposition for a
brief in which the five propositions given in the following
introduction shall be the five chief divisions of the argument : —

"A German who has seen the world and tries to make his
thinking free from the chance influences of his surroundings
may easily ask himself whether it would not be most desirable that all nations should become republican democracies
after the American model. If he does not ask the question
himself, he is sure to be asked it by an American friend who
happens not to agree with the last speech of the German
emperor, and who, therefore, takes for granted that an
educated German, outside of the reach of the German state
attorney, will frankly confess that monarchy is a mediæval
relic and that democracy alone is life. When one of my
friends approached me the other day with such an inquiry,
I was in a hurry, and my answers had to be short. I told
him, first, that the achievements of democratic America are
not the achievements of American democracy ; secondly,
that democracy in itself has as many bad tendencies as
good ones, and is thus not better than aristocracy ; thirdly,
that the question whether democracy or aristocracy is better
does not exist to-day ; fourthly, that Germany daily becomes more democratic, while America steadily grows aristocratic ; fifthly, that there is no difference between the two
nations anyway. My friend insisted that my argument stood
on the same level with the oath of the woman who was
accused before the court of breaking a pot which she had
borrowed from her neighbor, and she swore, first, that the

pot was not broken when she returned it; secondly, that
the pot was broken when she borrowed it; and thirdly, that
she had not borrowed the pot. Well, that may be ; but my
haste alone was to blame, as I could not explain in the few
words I had time for that democracy can cover very different tendencies. Thus I promised, when I had leisure, to dis-
entangle my twisted argument, and to illustrate, perhaps even
to establish it. The following remarks are, as far as possible,
a fulfillment of my promise, and they follow exactly the order
of the argument." — MÜNSTERBERG : *American Traits*.

2. Organize the following propositions into a brief to
prove the negative of the question, Would such saloons as
the Subway Tavern promote the cause of temperance in
New York City ?

They would not diminish the habit of drinking.

They would degrade moral standards.

They would not attract the hard drinkers.

They would not benefit those who drink moderately.

They would lure many who do not drink to form the
habit.

A hard drinker does not care for artistic furnishings.

A hard drinker is not fastidious about the quality of the
liquor he drinks if it is strong enough.

A hard drinker could find cheaper drink elsewhere.

The Christopher Slys do not know how to act in respectable surroundings.

They prefer what they are accustomed to.

A hard drinker wants quantity.

A hard drinker goes where he can get the most liquor for
his money.

He goes where there are no restrictions on the amount
he may drink.

Saloons operated on the plan of the Subway Tavern would have to charge good prices to make a profit.

They would sell pure liquor only.

They would offer no inducements for their patrons to buy more than one drink.

They would have high running expenses.

They would need a good building.

They would have to provide amusement.

They would have to employ trustworthy and capable attendants.

If a moderate drinker develops a taste for drink, he will leave the restricted saloon and go where he can get what he wants.

If a moderate drinker does not form a taste for drink, he has no need of such a saloon.

A moderate drinker will prefer other saloons.

There are many respectable saloons where the purchaser of one or two glasses of beer is welcome to sit throughout the evening.

There are many saloons with furnishings more pleasing to the ordinary drinking man's taste.

The moderate drinker resents the idea of supervision.

What is gaudy to the man of refined taste seems cheerful to the man whose taste is not cultivated.

What is harmonious to the man of refined taste seems dull and dreary to the uncultivated man.

The average poor drinking man does not want a saloon to which he can take his family.

He wants to get away from obligations.

He wants to escape claims on his sociability and his pocketbook.

He wants to escape criticism.

Such saloons would appeal to young men who had not the habit of drinking in public.

Such saloons would appeal to women.

Such saloons would prove an open door to degradation.

Such places are considered respectable.

Their club features are attractive.

They offer comfort and sociability and entertainment for a small fee.

The purchase of a cup of coffee or a mug of beer entitles a guest to an evening's entertainment.

The newcomer would soon fall into the habit of drinking.

He would be associated with drinking men.

He would feel it unpleasant to be different from others.

They make people think there is no wrong in the practice of drinking.

They make people think there is no wrong in selling intoxicating liquor for gain.

They make the beginner think that all men have self-control in drink.

They make the habitual drinker think that self-control is expected of no man.

They are founded on the assumption that men may drink whiskey in moderation.

They afford opportunity for a man to see his wife, his children, and his neighbors drinking spirituous liquors.

They afford opportunity for a man to see educated men and women drinking.

Educated people visit and patronize such places out of curiosity.

Habit brings him to excuse his friends and neighbors when they indulge to excess.

He soon comes to excuse over indulgence in himself.

Reform is not the sole motive of the " Tavern."

A large profit on the original investment is possible.

Dividends of five per cent are permitted.

The surplus is to be invested in similar profit-paying " Taverns."

Men of high social standing accept these profits.

3. What is the leading proposition in the following paragraph ?   Organize the proof in brief form.

" But that the main function of coloring is protection may be decided from the simplest observation of animal life in any part of the world.   Even among the larger animals, which one might suppose independent of subterfuge and whose appearance anywhere but in their native haunts suggests a very opposite theory, the harmony of color with environment is always more or less striking.   When we look, for instance, at the coat of a zebra, with its thunder-and-lightning pattern of black and white stripes, we should think such a conspicuous object designed to court rather than to elude attention.   But the effect in nature is just the opposite.   The black and white somehow take away the sense of a solid body altogether; the two colors seem to blend into the most inconspicuous gray, and at close quarters the effect is as of bars of light seen through the branches of shrubs.   I have found myself in the forest gazing at what I supposed to be a solitary zebra, its presence betrayed by some motion due to my approach, and suddenly realized that I was surrounded by an entire herd which were all invisible until they moved.   The motionlessness of wild game in the field when danger is near is well known ; and every hunter is aware of the difficulty of seeing even the largest animals, though they are standing just in front of him.

The tiger, whose stripes are obviously meant to imitate the reeds of the jungle in which it lurks, is nowhere found in Africa; but its beautiful cousin, the leopard, abounds in these forests, and its spotted pelt probably conveys the same sense of indistinctness as in the case of the zebra. The hippopotamus seems to find the deep water of the rivers — where it spends the greater portion of its time — a sufficient protection; but the crocodile is marvelously concealed by its knotted, mud-colored hide, and it is often quite impossible to tell at a distance whether the objects lying along the river banks are alligators or fallen logs." — HENRY DRUMMOND : *Tropical Africa*.

4. Reduce to brief form, giving the main proposition, the three propositions that support it, and the several propositions supporting them; supply reasons for the assertion, That the requirement that a member of Congress be a resident of the district that elects him, is due to the To-the-victor-belong-the-spoils system of civil service : —

" Our first aim should be, as it has been, the reform of our civil service, for that is the fruitful mother of all our ills. It is the most aristocratic system in the world, for it depends on personal favor and is the reward of personal service, and the power of the political boss is built up and maintained, like that of the mediæval robber baron, by his free-handedness in distributing the property of other people. From it is derived the notion that the public treasure is a fund to a share of which every one is entitled who by fraud or favor can get it, and from this again the absurd doctrine of rotation in office so that each may secure his proportion; and that the business of the nation may be carried on by a succession of apprentices who are dismissed, just as they are getting an inkling of their trade, to make room for others, who are in due time to be turned loose on the world, passed masters in nothing but in incompetence for any useful career. From this, too, has sprung the theory of the geographical allotment of patronage, as if ability were dependent, like wheat, upon the soil; and the more mischievous one, that members of Congress must be residents of the district that elects them, a custom which has sometimes excluded men of proved ability, in the full vigor of their faculties and the ripeness of their experience, from the councils of the nation." — JAMES R. LOWELL: *The Independent in Politics.*

5. Find the main proposition in the following argument; find the two chief supporting propositions, and organize the sustaining facts in brief form: —

"Sir, . . . as far as I am capable of discerning, there are but three ways of proceeding relative to this stubborn spirit which prevails in your colonies, and disturbs your government. These are: to change that spirit, as inconvenient, by removing the causes; to prosecute it as criminal; or to comply with it as necessary. I would not be guilty of an imperfect enumeration; I can think of but these three. Another has indeed been started, — that of giving up the colonies; but it met so slight a reception that I do not think myself obliged to dwell a great while upon it. It is nothing but a little sally of anger, like the frowardness of peevish children, who, when they cannot get all they would have, are resolved to take nothing.

"The first of these plans, to change the spirit, as inconvenient, by removing the causes, I think is the most like a systematic proceeding. It is radical in its principle; but it is attended with great difficulties, some of them little short, as I conceive, of impossibilities. This will appear by examining into the plans which have been proposed.

" As the growing population in the colonies is evidently one cause of their resistance, it was last session mentioned in both Houses, by men of weight, and received not without applause, that in order to check this evil, it would be proper for the crown to make no further grants of land. But to this scheme there are two objections. The first, that there is already so much unsettled land in private hands as to afford room for an immense future population, although the crown not only withheld its grants, but annihilated its soil. If this be the case, then the only effect of this avarice of desolation, this hoarding of a royal wilderness, would be to raise the value of the possessions in the hands of the great private monopolists, without any adequate check to the growing and alarming mischief of population.

" But if you stopped your grants, what would be the consequence? The people would occupy without grants. They have already so occupied in many places. You cannot station garrisons in every part of these deserts. If you drive the people from one place, they will carry on their annual tillage and remove with their flocks and herds to another. Many of the people in the back settlements are already little attached to particular situations. Already they have topped the Appalachian Mountains. From thence they behold before them an immense plain, one vast, rich, level meadow, a square of five hundred miles. Over this they would wander without a possibility of restraint; they would change their manners with the habits of their life; would soon forget a government by which they were disowned; would become hordes of English Tartars, and pouring down upon your unfortified frontiers a fierce and irresistible cavalry, become masters of your governors and your counsellors, your collectors and comptrollers, and of all the slaves that adhered to them. Such would, and in no long time must, be the effect of attempting to forbid as a crime, and to suppress as an evil, the command and blessing of providence, 'Increase and multiply.' Such would be the happy result of the endeavor to keep as a lair of wild beasts that earth which God, by an express charter, has given to the children of men. Far different and surely much wiser has been our policy hitherto. Hitherto we have invited our people, by every kind of bounty, to fixed establishments. We have invited the husbandman to look to authority for his title. We have taught him piously to believe in the mysterious virtue of wax and parchment. We have thrown each tract of land, as it was peopled, into districts, that the ruling power should never be wholly out of sight. We have settled all we could, and we have carefully attended every settlement with government.

"Adhering, Sir, as I do, to this policy, as well as for the reasons I have just given, I think this new project of hedging-in population to be neither prudent nor practicable.

"To impoverish the colonies in general, and in particular to arrest the noble course of their marine enterprises, would be a more easy task. I freely confess it. We have shown a disposition to a system of this kind, — a disposition even to continue the restraint after the offense, looking on ourselves as rivals to our colonies, and persuaded that of course we must gain all that they shall lose. Much mischief we may certainly do. The power inadequate to all other things is often more than sufficient for this. I do not look on the direct and immediate power of the colonies to resist our violence as very formidable. In this, however, I may be mistaken. But when I consider that we have colonies for no purpose but to be serviceable to us, it seems to my poor understanding a little preposterous to make them unserviceable in order to keep them obedient. It is, in truth, nothing more than the old and, as I thought, exploded problem of tyranny, which proposes to beggar its subjects into submission. But remember, when you have completed your system of impoverishment, that Nature still proceeds in her ordinary course; that discontent will increase with misery; and that there are critical moments in the fortune of all states, when they who are too weak to contribute to your prosperity may be strong enough to complete your ruin. *Spoliatis arma supersunt.*

" The temper and character which prevail in our colonies are, I am afraid, unalterable by any human art. We cannot, I fear, falsify the pedigree of this fierce people and persuade them that they are not sprung from a nation in whose veins the blood of freedom circulates. The language in which they would hear you tell them this tale would detect the imposition; your speech would betray you. An Englishman is the unfittest person on earth to argue another Englishman into slavery.

" I think it is nearly as little in our power to change their republican religion as their free descent, or to substitute the Roman Catholic as a penalty, or the Church of England as an improvement. The mode of inquisition and dragooning is going out of fashion in the Old World, and I should not confide much to their efficacy in the New. The education of the Americans is also on the same unalterable bottom with their religion. You cannot persuade them to burn their books of curious science, to banish their lawyers from their courts of laws, or to quench the lights of their assemblies by refusing to choose those persons who are best read in their privileges. It would be no less impracticable to think of wholly annihilating the popular assemblies in which these lawyers sit. The army, by which we must govern in their place, would be far more chargeable to us; not quite so effectual; and perhaps in the end full as difficult to be kept in obedience.

"With regard to the high aristocratic spirit of Virginia and the southern colonies, it has been proposed, I know, to reduce it by declaring a general enfranchisement of their slaves. This project has had its advocates and panegyrists; yet I never could argue myself into any opinion of it. Slaves are often much attached to their masters. A general wild offer of liberty would not always be accepted. History furnishes few instances of it. It is sometimes as hard to persuade slaves to be free, as it is to compel freemen to be slaves; and in this auspicious scheme we should have both these pleasing tasks on our hands at once. But when we talk of enfranchisement, do we not perceive that the American master may enfranchise too, and arm servile hands in defense of freedom? — a measure to which other people have had recourse more than once, and not without success, in a desperate situation of their affairs.

"Slaves as these unfortunate black people are, and dull as all men are from slavery, must they not a little suspect the offer of freedom from that very nation which has sold them to their present masters? from that nation, one of whose causes of quarrel with those masters is their refusal to deal any more in that inhuman traffic? An offer of freedom from England would come rather oddly, shipped to them in an African vessel, which is refused an entry into the

ports of Virginia or Carolina with a cargo of three hundred
Angola negroes. It would be curious to see the Guinea
captain attempting at the same instant to publish his proclamation of liberty, and to advertise his sale of slaves.

"But let us suppose all these moral difficulties got over.
The ocean remains. You cannot pump this dry; and as
long as it continues in its present bed, so long all the causes
which weaken authority by distance will continue.

> ' Ye gods, annihilate but space and time,
> And make two lovers happy!'

was a pious and passionate prayer; but just as reasonable
as many of the serious wishes of grave and solemn politi-
cians.

"If then, Sir, it seems almost desperate to think of any
alterative course for changing the moral causes (and not
quite easy to remove the natural) which produce prejudices
irreconcilable to the late exercise of our authority, but
that the spirit infallibly will continue; and continuing, will
produce such effects as now embarrass us, — the second
mode under consideration is to prosecute that spirit in
its overt acts as *criminal*." — BURKE : *Conciliation with the
Colonies*.

THE QUANTITY OF EVIDENCE

All parts of a brief must be correctly related, but a
brief that is absolutely coherent, and correct in form,
may fail totally as an argument. The failure may be
due to insufficient evidence.

Evidence is insufficient when there are not enough
lines of argument worked out to sustain the main prop-

osition, or when a line of argument is not carried far enough. There must be enough supporting propositions, and each of them must be firmly established. Each pier of the bridge of argument must rest on bed rock, and there must be piers enough.

The error of not having enough supporting propositions should be carefully guarded against. Each proposition, with the proposition or propositions supporting it, forms a contracted syllogism or enthymeme. From the conclusion and premise given the other premise is easily inferred, and the syllogism completed. Where the reasons are insufficient the middle term is inexact, and the major premise is accordingly not admissible.

When we assert that Whittier's poems show him to have been an Abolitionist, for

I. His poems show him to have been deeply interested in the antislavery movement;

and proceed to establish the truth of the proposition, *His poems show him to have been deeply interested in the antislavery movement*, without offering other coördinate reasons to prove that he was an Abolitionist, we imply the following syllogism : —

All men who were deeply interested in the antislavery movement were Abolitionists.

Whittier was deeply interested in the antislavery movement.

Whittier was an Abolitionist.

The major premise of this proposition is, however, not tenable, since the slaveholders themselves must have felt a keen interest in a movement so important to them. If, then, we add a second reason, *Whittier's poems show him to have believed that slavery was wrong*, what of the major premise? The middle term will then be, *All men who were deeply interested in the antislavery movement and believed slavery to be wrong*. The resulting major premise is still unsatisfactory, for not all men who were deeply interested in the antislavery movement and believed slavery to be wrong were Abolitionists. Lincoln was such a man and he was not an Abolitionist as distinguished from a Republican.

If we add a third reason, *For he gave the movement his support*, we shall have the following syllogism:

All men who were deeply interested in the antislavery movement, who believed slavery to be wrong, and who gave their support to the abolition movement were Abolitionists.

Whittier was a man who was deeply interested in the antislavery movement, believed slavery to be wrong, and gave his support to the abolition movement.

Whittier was an Abolitionist.

At last we have a satisfactory middle term and consequently an admissible major premise.

One reasons, The Indians were not driven from Florida against their wish, for a treaty agreeing to their removal had been signed by leading Seminoles. Evidence that such a treaty had been made is, of course, wanted; but that fact, however firmly established, is insufficient to prove that the Indians were not driven from Florida against their will. An added fact must be proved; the treaty must be shown to have been signed by an adequate representation of the Seminoles, acting understandingly and without bribery or coercion.

At every step through the argument the test of whether or not there is enough collateral evidence is the implied major premise. Do the coördinate propositions taken together imply a tenable major premise? Have we enough reasons for maintaining that Whittier was deeply interested in the anti-slavery movement? Take for reasons,

A. He gave much attention to the question.
B. His was an enduring interest.
C. His was a heartfelt interest.

The major premise suggested by these propositions is, All men who give much attention to a question, who have an enduring interest in it, and a heartfelt interest in it, are men who are deeply interested in a question. This seems a proposition that would be granted by both sides. The base for the argument is broad enough.

On the other hand, the error of allowing the proposition to rest at last on nothing substantial, on unproved assertion, is frequent. We are amused at the naïveté of people who accounted for the support of the earth by saying it rested on the back of an elephant, and that the elephant stood on a tortoise, and were content without inquiring what supported the tortoise. We laugh when the child complacently answers the question, What makes the automobile go? "The wheels." Yet in the informal and the formal discourse of more sophisticated people we frequently discover as great simplicity; the removal of the mystery one step is taken as its solution.

The assertion that Whittier's poetry shows him to have been an Abolitionist, for

I. His poems show that he was deeply interested in the antislavery movement.

II. His poems show that he believed that slavery was wrong in theory.

III. His poems show that he supported the antislavery movement as a practical measure;

does not prove that the main proposition is true. It rests merely upon generalizations that themselves need proof. It is necessary to prove each of these. While the propositions, that

A. The question received much of his attention,

B. The question received his enduring interest,

C. The question received his heart-felt interest,

offer a sufficiently broad base for proof that Whittier was deeply interested, they do not penetrate deeply enough. Each in turn will have to be sustained by evidence. This process must be carried on till the proposition rests on facts or on accepted principles. Until such a foundation is reached we have not proof, but mere assertion. The evidence we offer needs evidence. We must not stop before we have discovered the support of the tortoise.

There must, then, be enough piers to the bridge of argument, and they must be grounded on the bed rock of facts. Further, these piers must be of sufficient height and strength. The proposition that is the subject of discussion may not rest immediately on the ultimate evidence. The intermediate steps must be taken. One may not argue that Whittier's poems show him to have been an Abolitionist, for he wrote in his poems : and proceed to quote antislavery sentiments from Whittier's poetry. The work of arguing includes the sifting of evidence and its interpretation. It is the business of the arguer to show the significance and the bearing of the facts he cites, to build up a high enough pile of consecutive argument between the facts and the proposition, without any flaw, or break, or twist. Often when confronted with the facts that ultimately prove a proposition, we are as blind to their import as was Legrand's friend in the following instance : —

" Upon persevering in the experiment, there became visible at the corner of the slip, diagonally opposite to the spot in which the death's-head was delineated, the figure of what I at first supposed to be a goat. A closer scrutiny, however, satisfied me that it was intended for a kid.

"'Ha! ha!' said I, 'to be sure I have no right to laugh at you, — a million and a half of money is too serious a matter for mirth, — but you are not about to establish a third link in your chain : you will not find any especial connection between your pirates and a goat ; pirates, you know, have nothing to do with goats ; they appertain to the farming interest.'

"'But I have just said that the figure was *not* that of a goat.'

"'Well, a kid, then — pretty much the same thing.'

"'Pretty much, but not altogether,' said Legrand. 'You may have heard of one *Captain* Kidd.' I at once looked on the figure of the animal as a kind of punning or hieroglyphical signature. I say signature ; because its position upon the vellum suggested the idea." — Poe : *The Gold Bug.*

Be sure in drawing a brief to have enough lines of argument, to establish each firmly, and to see that there is no missing link in the chain of reasoning.

This teaching, if closely followed without discrimination, may lead the student into error. Those who are anxious to meet the requirements of argument rather than to prove a point, often assiduously strive merely to cover the ground, to leave nothing without giving acceptable evidence of it. The result is sure to be ineffective. All parts of the argument should not, as a rule, be developed with uniform elaborateness. What is obvious or unessential does not have to be proved with the care that must be given to the less apparent and the more important points.

In the example already cited, one could not prove Whittier to have been an Abolitionist without proving him to have supported abolition as a practical measure. But elaborately to prove propositions I and II, that he was interested in and sympathized with the antislavery movement, would be folly, since proposition III implies I and II. A man's interest and sympathy in a measure he supports will usually be granted without much argument. His support to the movement is the main point, and there the stress of the argument should rest.

Emphasis and proportion are as important to the success of an argument as thoroughness.

EXERCISES

1. Tell why the following enthymemes are not convincing : —

a. *Enoch Arden* is a beautiful poem, for Tennyson wrote it.

b. Dickens was a greater novelist than Thackeray, for his novels are more interesting.

c. He is an educated man, because he is well informed.

d. *Death in the Desert* is a more profound poem than *Saul*, for *Death in the Desert* was written when Browning was older.

e. He is a Democrat, for he spoke with admiration of Grover Cleveland.

f. Washington was not so great a benefactor to his country as Jefferson, for he was not a statesman.

g. It must have been about ten o'clock, for the sun was just beginning to shine into the west windows.

h. If the war is a long one, the Russians will win, for they have more endurance than the Japanese.

i. As one of the most severe critics in town is pleased with the statue, every one will like it.

j. The Salvation Army is more deserving of support than the churches, for it does more good.

k. The book can have no merit, for its author was an immoral man.

2. What is the proposition to be proved in the following speech ? Is it proved ? If not, why not ?

"If there be any in this assembly, any dear friend of Cæsar's, to him I say that Brutus' love to Cæsar was no less than his. If then that friend demand why Brutus rose against Cæsar, this is my answer : — Not that I loved Cæsar less, but that I loved Rome more. Had you rather Cæsar were living, and die all slaves, than that Cæsar were dead, to live all free men? As Cæsar loved me, I weep for him ; as he was fortunate, I rejoice at it ; as he was valiant, I honor him : but, as he was ambitious, I slew him. There is tears for his love ; joy for his fortune ; honor for his valor ; and death for his ambition. Who is here so base that would be a bondman? If any, speak ; for him have I offended. Who is here so rude that would not be a Roman? If any, speak ; for him have I offended. Who is here so vile that will not love his country? If any, speak ; for him have I offended." — SHAKESPEARE : *Julius Cæsar*.

3. Consider the following as material for an argument on the thesis, *Russia should not pay the indemnity asked by*

Japan. Put the argument into brief form. What is its weakness ? What is the proposition it proves ?

WHY THE CZAR REFUSES TO PAY

PORTSMOUTH, N. H., August 18.

" Mr. de Martens, one of the Russian delegates and recognized as one of the great authorities on international law, not only in Russia, but throughout the world, in speaking about the principle of the war indemnity, said that there was no precedent in history where a country whose territory was not occupied in whole or in part by the enemy, had paid war tribute upon the conclusion of peace.

" Russia, Mr. de Martens said, was not crushed. She was not on her knees begging for peace. She wanted peace, but she could go on fighting for years. Japan had not even approached the true Russian frontier.

" ' Should Russia consent to pay tribute to Japan in any form,' continued the eminent jurist, ' it would be her political death. The powers would understand that she accepted the proposition of President Roosevelt, not because she was desirous of an honorable peace, but because her power had been annihilated and she recognized that it was impossible for her to continue the war. It would mean a public confession that Russia is at Portsmouth helplessly kneeling before Japan, imploring peace and ready to accept any terms imposed. No one will seriously contend that the Muscovite empire is in any such position.'

" With many interesting historical examples Mr. de Martens proceeded to elaborate his thesis that no country ever had paid indemnity except when powerless to confront the enemy on the field of battle and with a large portion of her territory in the enemy's possession as a hostage.

" In 1807, he pointed out, when Napoleon imposed the peace of Tilsit, French troops occupied practically all of Prussia and the Prussian royal family had fled to Russian soil. France could dictate terms. She exacted a war indemnity of $300,000,000 and garrisoned several Prussian towns with French troops at the expense of Prussia as a guarantee of payment. She required that the Prussian army should be reduced to 40,000 men.

" In 1815, when Napoleon was annihilated at Waterloo after the famous ' 100 days,' and the second treaty of Paris was concluded, the allied powers, occupying Paris as the Prussians did later in 1870, imposed in addition to other conditions a war indemnity of $500,000,000 to be paid in five years, during which time the allied troops were to hold a portion of French territory. That sum, however, was considerably reduced by Lord Wellington at Aix-la-Chapelle, and France completed the payment of the indemnity in three years.

" The largest war indemnity ever exacted was imposed by Prince Bismarck upon France in 1870. It amounted to $1,000,000,000. But Napoleon III had fallen. Gambetta was powerless. Prussia was at Paris. The third republic succeeded in liquidating the indemnity in two years, while, according to the treaty, she had five years' time in which to pay.

" In other cases, even where a portion of the territory of the fated country was occupied, no indemnity was exacted, or even asked. For instance, Russia, in 1856, although the Crimean peninsula was occupied by the Anglo-Franco-Piedmontese troops, was not asked to pay tribute. Neither was Austria, in 1859, after having lost Lombardy, nor in 1866, after having been beaten by Prussia. Denmark, in 1864, lost Schleswig-Holstein to Prussia, but paid nothing.

" ' A new precedent was made by America,' added Mr. de Martens, ' in her war with Spain. Although victorious and in a position to claim indemnity, she ended the war on principle, and actually paid $20,000,000 to the Madrid government for the Philippine Islands.

" ' But that,' he remarked, ' was, as the French say, to *dorer la pilule.*'

" Independent of all these considerations, Mr. de Martens said, Russia's objection to the payment of an indemnity, no matter under what form, comes from the fact that in all her history she never paid a cent tribute to a foreign power, not even during the time of her worst defeats under Peter the Great, when a large portion of the country was in the hands of the invader. In conclusion, he called attention to the fact that to pay an indemnity to Japan would be for Russia to create a precedent new in the world's history."

4. Classify the evidence in the following and indicate clearly, step by step, how apparently inconsistent facts are related to the proposition, Horace Roberts should have a college education : —

His father is a mechanic.

His father earns only $2 a day.

Horace's back is weak.

He has an invalid sister.

He has acted as his sister's tutor.

His uncle has influence.

His uncle is rich.

His uncle is stingy.

His mother was a successful school-teacher before she married.

His father has no education.

His father never keeps a position long.

Horace led his class in high school.

He was considered the best writer in his class.

Though repeatedly asked to write for school papers, he refused.

He refused to enter the interclass debate.

He refused to run for class president.

Horace often worked at his lessons till after midnight.

He fainted after taking his last examination.

5. What proposition is proved by the following paragraph? What broader proposition does the writer assume that he is establishing? What is wanting for its proof? Why does the writer content himself with giving evidence to prove only one of the two propositions whose truth is essential to the truth of the proposition he advocates?

"There was no sort of selection of these boys, or any others who were brought up by us to one or other branch of Mr. Morris's business. John Smith, who is now the dyer at Merton, was taken into the dyeshop because it was just being set up at the time he was getting too old to remain errand boy. Dearle was put to the tapestry because that business then wanted an apprentice; and so of the other two. They were put to the loom because at the time we were starting this we were asked to do something for them. We took Sleath on that ground first of all, and he introduced Knight. The same rule applied to all others, and its working justified Mr. Morris's contention that the universal modern system, which he called that of Devil take the hindmost, is frightfully wasteful of human intelligence. A few years later, when we were able to set up a third tapestry loom, we found a lad with equal facility, without selection of any kind — the nephew of the housekeeper at Merton.

She happened to tell me, at the time we were getting the new loom ready, that her nephew had left school and was looking for something to do." — J. W. MACKAIL : *Life of William Morris.*

6. The following propositions are in the working order recommended on page 95. Rearrange in brief form : —

Whittier's poems show him to have been an Abolitionist.

Whittier's poems show him to have been deeply interested in the antislavery movement.

Whittier's poems show him to have believed that slavery was wrong and that emancipation was right in theory.

Whittier's poems show that he favored abolition as a practical measure.

They show that the question of slavery claimed a large share of his attention.

They show that with him the antislavery question was an enduring interest.

They show that it was a heartfelt interest.

There are more than ninety poems among the so-called *Antislavery Poems.*

These do not include many poems that sprang from his interest in the question of slavery.

Many of his poems on other subjects contain allusions to slavery.

They do not include *Brown of Ossawatomie, Ichabod,* etc.

All are familiar with the reference to slavery in *Snow-Bound* in the characterization of the schoolmaster.

In *The Mayflowers* we find : —

> "The Pilgrim's wild and wintry day
>   Its shadow round us draws ;
> The Mayflower of his stormy bay,
>   Our Freedom's struggling cause," etc.

In *The Last Walk in Autumn* Whittier declares his preference for—

> "The painted, shingly town-house where
> The freeman's vote for Freedom falls!"

and says:—

> "I have not seen, I may not see,
> My hopes for man take form in fact,
> But God will give the victory
> In due time; in that faith I act."

In *The Prisoners of Naples* he says:—

> "I, who have spoken for freedom at the cost
> Of some weak friendships, or some paltry prize
> Of name or place," etc.

In *What the Voice Said* we find:—

> "With the brute the man is sold," etc.

In *Astræa, After Election, Our Country, The Ship-builders, The Reformer,* and many other poems there are references made to slavery in America.

They show that in the early days of the antislavery movement he took an interest in the question.

They show that when troubled times came his interest did not abate.

They show that after emancipation was accomplished he retained his interest.

In 1832 he addressed a poem to Garrison declaring his admiration for him and interest in his work.

Some of his most notable antislavery poetry was written before the Mexican War.

Toussaint L'Ouverture, Moral Warfare, The Farewell of a Virginia Slave Mother, Massachusetts to Virginia, To

Faneuil Hall, Texas: Voice of New England, and others, belong to this period.

The significant episodes during the stormy times of the antislavery struggle called forth verses from Whittier.

Calhoun's opposition to the acquisition of Oregon was marked by *To a Southern Statesman*.

Randolph's death furnished occasion for pointing a moral in *Randolph of Roanoke*.

The significance of the treaty with Mexico was emphasized by *The Crisis*.

The attempts to carry out the Fugitive Slave Law and their results gave occasion for such poems as *A Sabbath Scene, Moloch in State Street, The Rendition, Arisen at Last.*

The squatter sovereignty struggles gave opportunity for *The Kansas Emigrants, The Burial of Barber, Le Marais du Cygne.*

The apostasy of Webster stirred Whittier to write *Ichabod*.

The execution of John Brown called forth the poem, *Brown of Ossawatomie*.

" *Ein Feste Burg ist unser Gott*," *The Battle Autumn of 1862, Barbara Frietchie*, etc., are familiar war poems.

He celebrated the emancipation proclamation with *The Proclamation*.

He celebrated the passage of the emancipation amendment with *Laus Deo !*

After the war he wrote *The Peace Autumn, The Thirty-Ninth Congress, To the Emancipation Group, Garrison.*

Most of the antislavery poems are serious.

Many of the antislavery poems show strong emotion.

Such poems as *A Letter, Letter from a Missionary, The Hunters of Men*, etc., are the exception.

Even these have a certain grimness in their humor.

The sarcasm of *The Hunters of Men* is not mirth-provoking.

Such poems as *Expostulation, Clerical Oppressors, The Sentence of John L. Brown, To Faneuil Hall, Ichabod,* express righteous indignation.

The Farewell of a Virginia Slave Mother shows sympathy and tenderness.

" *Ein Feste Burg* " expresses firm patience in suffering.

Laus Deo ! expresses solemn joy.

Whittier's antislavery poems are frequently in the form of hymns or invocations.

Whittier's antislavery poems are full of appeals to patriotic and religious sentiment.

Hymn : O Thou, whose Presence went Before, Clerical Oppressors, Hymn: O Holy Father ! just and true, Lines from a Letter to a Young Clerical Friend, Thy Will be Done, etc., etc., are altogether addressed to Deity.

Almost every one of the antislavery poems contains some reference to Deity.

Allusions to the delivery of the children of Israel are frequent. We find : —

"The storm . . . which wasted Egypt's earth."— *Stanzas.*

"The songs of grateful millions rise
Like that of Israel's ransomed band." — *The New Year.*

". . . the mystic rod,
Of old stretched o'er the Egyptian wave.
Which opened in the strength of God,
A pathway for the slave." — *The Relic.*

"Sing with Miriam by the sea,
He has cast the mighty down ;
Horse and rider sink and drown ;
He hath triumphed gloriously ! " — *Laus Deo!*

Whittier's antislavery poems show that he disapproved of slavery in the abstract.

They show that he had personal sympathy for the negro slaves.

They show that he looked upon negro slavery as injurious to the slaveholder.

He looked upon slavery as morally wrong.

He opposed slavery in all ages and places.

He regarded the negro as " brother-man, and fellow-countryman."

He was sensible to the horrors of slavery to the slave.

Such passages as the following are common in his anti-slavery poetry : —

> " What, ho ! our countrymen in chains !
>   The whip on woman's shrinking flesh !
>   Our soil yet reddening with the stains
>   Caught from her scourging, warm and fresh !
>   What ! mothers from their children riven !
>   What ! God's own image bought and sold !
>   Americans to market driven,
>   And bartered as the brute for gold." — *Stanzas*.

In *The Peace of Europe* Whittier denounces tyranny and slavery, however disguised.

In *To Pius IX* he denounces tyranny in the church.

In *The New Exodus* he rejoices over the report of the abolition of slavery in Egypt.

In *Freedom in Brazil* he rejoices over the liberation of slaves.

The Farewell of a Virginia Slave Mother, *The Song of Slaves in the Desert*, and other poems mentioning the suffering of the slave, show that sympathy and imagination, as well as reason, were responsible for Whittier's opposition to slavery.

He put himself in their place.

He said to the Virginia slaveholders : —

> "Plant, if ye will, your fathers' graves with rankest
> weeds of shame."

Again, to the slaveholder he says : —

> "And the curse of unpaid toil,
> Downward through your generous soil
> Like a fire shall burn and spoil," etc.

He saw that it brutalized the southern women.

He saw that it made the churchmen traitors to their trust.

Whittier's poems show that he approved the abolitionist leaders and their measures.

They show him to have been identified with the movement.

They show that he thought abolition should be gained at any price.

Whittier shows his admiration for the friends of freedom in *Garrison*, *To the Memory of Thomas Shipley*, *Ritner*, *The Branded Hand*, *Daniel Neall*, *The Lost Statesman*, *To John C. Frémont*, etc., etc.

Many of Whittier's occasional poems, together with the occasion that called them forth, have been already named.

The publication of poems of this nature committed their author to the cause he advocated.

Some of the poems show Whittier to have taken part in specific abolition measures.

Many of the poems were intended to excite sympathy and rouse to action.

Pennsylvania Hall was written for the dedication of the hall of that name to the cause of freedom.

They show that, patriot though he was, he thought disunion not too great a price to pay for deliverance from a share in the responsibility of slaveholding.

They show that, Quaker though he was, he thought war was not too great a price to pay for freedom.

They show that he thought that existing evils could be stopped through abolition.

In *Texas: Voice of New England* he wrote : —

" Take your slavery-blackened vales ;
    Leave us but our own free gales,
    Blowing on our thousand sails.

    Boldly, or with treacherous art,
    Strike the blood-wrought chain apart ;
    Break the Union's mighty heart."

In *A Word for the Hour* he wrote :—

"They break the links of Union :
    *   *   *   *   *   *
Draw we not even now a freer breath,
As from our shoulders falls a load of death.
    *   *   *   *   *   *
Why take we up the accursed thing again?
Pity, forgive, but urge them back no more
Who, drunk with passion, flaunt disunion's rag
With its vile reptile-blazon.   Let us press
The golden cluster on our brave old flag
In closer union, and, if numbering less,
Brighter shall shine the stars that still remain."

In *To Faneuil Hall* he wrote : —

" Have they wronged us?   Let us then
      Render back nor threats nor prayers ;
Have they chained our free-born men?
      Let us unchain theirs !

Up, your banner leads the van,
　　Blazoned, 'Liberty for all!'
Finish what your sires began!
　　Up, to Faneuil Hall!"

While war was in progress, in 1862, he wrote: —

"Not as we hoped; but what are we?
　　Above our broken dreams and plans
　　God lays, with wiser hand than man's
The corner-stones of liberty.
I cavil not with Him: the voice
　　That freedom's blessed gospel tells
　　Is sweet to me as silver bells,
Rejoicing! yea, I will rejoice!"
　　　　　　　　　　— *Astræa at the Capitol.*

In *Ein Feste Burg ist unser Gott* he wrote: —

"What gives the wheat-field blades of steel?
　　What points the rebel cannon?
What sets the roaring rabble's heel
　　On the old star-spangled pennon?
　　What breaks the oath
　　Of the men o' the South?
　　What whets the knife
　　For the Union's life? —
Hark to the answer: Slavery!

*　　　*　　　*　　　*　　　*　　　*

In vain the bells of war shall ring
　　Of triumphs and revenges,
While still is spared the evil thing
　　That severs and estranges."

7. Point out the virtues and the defects in the brief into which you have organized the proposition given above.

THE KIND OF EVIDENCE

Where it is important to impress the reader with the truth of a proposition, it is well not to depend on one line of argument, however strong that may seem. Give the proposition manifold proof. Let one argument reënforce another. Make assurance doubly sure. Not to weary the reader with repetition, have recourse to arguments of various kinds.

We may offer as evidence facts gained from our own experience or observation, or from the observation of others; or we may offer opinions or inferences, our own opinions grounded on our own observations or on the observations or the opinions of others, or the opinions of others grounded on their own observations or on the observations or the opinions of others.

We usually trust the evidence of our own senses, but even that is not absolutely reliable: the eye or the ear reports the appearance rather than the fact; if you whirl a burning stick, you see what appears to be an unbroken ring of fire; the white cow may look purple in a certain light; the skiff seems repeated in the clear water; the answering call is but an echo; appearances often deceive. And again we see not what really appears but what we expect to see — fevered fancy converts the white-trunked sycamore into a ghost for Ichabod Crane — yet on the whole we trust our senses.

Furthermore, we are constantly making inferences and acting upon them with confidence; yet they are by no means infallible. We hourly make use of the *a priori* argument; that is, the argument that something will happen because something has happened, that it will rain because the clouds have gathered, that it will thunder because it has lightened, that there will be a good harvest because the blossoms are abundant, that I shall find *Romola* interesting because I have found *The Mill on the Floss* interesting.

We as frequently use the *a posteriori* argument, that something must have happened because something else has happened since, that it was cold last night because the lake is frozen, that the soil is rich because the corn flourishes, that there is a fire because there is smoke; Crusoe's argument that a man had been on his island because there was a man's footprint in the sand, was of this kind.

We also put our faith in argument by analogy or likeness; we see a silent, ponderous man and we say, " Still waters run deep," and expect great things of him; when a friend consults us about making another change in business, we look dubious and say, " A rolling stone gathers no moss." The student says, "a brief only hinders me in writing," and the instructor replies, " David learned to wear the armor of Saul."

Inferences are nevertheless not sure; all signs fail in dry weather; the bloom may be blighted; the light that promises the wanderer welcome may prove a will-o'-the-wisp; a man may smile and smile and be a villain.

Various inferences are frequently drawn from the same facts. An amusing instance of this recently occurred in a western town : —

In the stone work over the door of an apartment house that was being erected on a prominent street appeared the word *Coredjo*. Immediately a citizen wrote a letter to the public through an evening paper, calling attention to the name of the house and commenting that it was strange that a man of sufficient culture to care for the art of *Correggio* should be so ignorant as to blunder so conspicuously in the spelling of his name. This man's reasoning was, All men who spell *Correggio, Coredjo*, are ignorant of how it should be spelled.

This man spelled *Correggio, Coredjo*.

This man is ignorant of how it should be spelled.

The next night a second letter was published, referring to the first letter and asserting that this was evidently not a case of ignorance, but a virulent case of spelling reform mania, and regretting that a man who had sufficient sentiment to wish to pay tribute to an artist by naming a house for him should have so little right reverence for him as to take such vulgar liberties with his name. This writer made it clear that the major premise of the first reasoner was not reliable by showing that all men who misspelled *Correggio* were not necessarily ignorant of the conventional spelling. He would substitute as the major premise of his syllogism, All men who deliberately spell *Correggio, Coredjo*, are spelling reform maniacs. At last a letter from the builder of the house appeared, showing that it was the minor premise that was at fault; he was not a man who spelled *Correggio*, *Coredjo*; he did not know of the existence of *Correggio*; the name of his house was a word made up of the first syllables of the names of his three children. The two letter writers had made the same blunder: they had generalized that all men who employ a combination of letters that gives the pronunciation of *Correggio's* name intend his name — a blunder that most of us would have made.

The evidence of our own senses, and our own inferences from our own observations, are usually the most convincing proof to us. But, however much we trust our own senses and power to make correct inferences, we often rightly yield to the judgment of another. The child accepts its father's assurance that the trees and the fences are not rushing past the train windows; the man crossing the desert trusts the guide's wisdom when the latter tells him the inviting palms he so plainly sees are but a mirage; we give up our own theories and yield to the doctor's verdict. Where one is by nature or training a more trustworthy observer or reasoner than his fellows, we often accept his opinion without question, even when it conflicts with our own. But even where the authority is recognized and admitted to be most competent, the active mind demands grounds for the conclusion suggested; it refuses to hold an opinion merely because some one else holds it.

The argument by authority is not so convincing and conclusive as most young writers seem to think. Many seem to hold the conviction that whatever appears in print is, *ipso facto*, true, and such students offer quoted opinions as sufficient evidence of a proposition that needs proof. Quotation marks alone do not give weight to an assertion. The reader must know whose opinion is offered that he may decide whether or not he is entitled to speak with authority. We are not always able to take at its full value the testimony of one to whose personal advantage it would be to have the belief he advocates prevail. We find it necessary to discount the opinion of the prejudiced. The woolen manufacturer's assurance that the prices on woolen goods are reasonably low is not going to be accepted by the farmer without supporting statistics. The mine operator's opinion that immigration should not be restricted, the capitalist's conviction that the closed shop is a social evil, are supposed a little to savor of the logic of the wolf who complained that the lamb was muddling the water.

The authority cited must not only be disinterested, it must be competent to pronounce upon the subject under discussion. Certain authorities are conceded by some to be almost incontestable, as the Century Dictionary is to many in matters of pronunciation, the Constitution of the United States in matters of legislation, the Bible in matters religious. The opinion of a distinguished specialist has weight as evidence. While, then, the conclusion without the name of the person holding it avails little or nothing as evidence, the reminder that several eminent authorities sustain you in your opinion has weight.

It is, however, more effective for the sake of convincing the reader not merely to give the conclusion, but to tell the facts or the reasons upon which the conclusion is based. Macaulay might have planned his paragraph on the bad roads of England thus : —

I. The roads in England were at this time in bad condition, for
> *A.* They are so reported by Thoresby in his *Diary*.
> *B.* They are so reported by Pepys in his *Diary*.

But he chose to fill out *A* and *B* with a recital of the specific instances upon which the conclusion was based, as follows : —

" Those highways appear to have been far worse than might have been expected from the degree of wealth and civilization which the nation had even then attained. On the best lines of communication the ruts were deep, the descents precipitous, and the way often such as it was hardly possible to distinguish, in the dusk, from the uninclosed heath and fen which lay on both sides. Ralph Thoresby, the antiquary, was in danger of losing his way on the great North road, between Barnby Moor and Tuxford, and actually lost his way between Doncaster and York.[1] Pepys and his wife,

[1] Thoresby's *Diary*, Oct. 21, 1680, Aug. 3, 1712.

traveling in their own coach, lost their way between Newbury
and Reading. In the course of the same tour they lost
their way near Salisbury, and were in danger of having to
pass the night on the plain.[1] It was only in fine weather
that the whole breadth of the road was available for wheeled
vehicles. Often the mud lay deep on the right and the left;
and only a narrow track of firm ground rose above the quag-
mire.[2] At such times obstructions and quarrels were frequent, and the path was sometimes blocked up during a long
time by carriers, neither of whom would break the way. It
happened, almost every day, that coaches stuck fast, until a
team of cattle could be procured from some neighboring
farm, to tug them out of the slough. But in bad seasons
the traveler had to encounter inconveniences still more
serious. Thoresby, who was in the habit of traveling between Leeds and the capital, has recorded in his *Diary* such
a series of perils and disasters as might suffice for a journey to
the Frozen Ocean or to the Desert of Sahara. On one occasion he learned that the floods were out between Ware and
London, that passengers had to swim for their lives, and that
a higgler had perished in the attempt to cross. In consequence of these tidings he turned out of the highroad, and
was conducted across some meadows, where it was necessary
for him to ride to the saddle skirts in water.[3] In the course
of another journey he narrowly escaped being swept away
by an inundation of the Trent. He was afterwards detained
at Stamford four days on account of the state of the roads,
and then ventured to proceed only because fourteen members of the House of Commons, who were going up in a

[1] Pepys's *Diary*, June 12 and 16, 1668.
[2] *Ibid.*, Feb. 28, 1660.
[3] Thoresby's *Diary*, May 17, 1695.

body to Parliament with guides and numerous attendants, took him into their company.[1] "

— MACAULAY : History of England.

Had Miss Puffer, in The Psychology of Beauty, told us that Bernard of Clairvaux, Eckhart, St. Teresa, Keats, and Schopenhauer testified to "the fading of consciousness of self as feeling nears the white heat," the reader familiar with the utterances of those named would have demanded nothing more, but even he is glad to have his memory further aided by such a passage as : —

" . . . in all the stages of religious ecstasy, æsthetic pleasure, and creative inspiration, is to be traced what we know as the loss of the feeling of self.   Bernard of Clairvaux dwells on 'that ecstasy of deification in which the individual disappears in the eternal essence as the drop of water in a cask of wine.'   Says Meister Eckhart, 'Thou shalt sink away from thy selfhood, thou shalt flow into his self-possession, the very thought of Thine shall melt into His Mine'; and St. Teresa, 'The soul, in thus searching for its God, feels with a very lively and very sweet pleasure that it is fainting almost quite away,'" etc.— PUFFER : The Psychology of Beauty.

If the witness cited is not widely known, it is well to give his full name and in addition to give some reason why he should be regarded as reliable.

To be sure, in using the argument of authority it is not always necessary or wise, besides naming the authorities, to give their grounds for belief and the

<hr />

[1] Thoresby's Diary, Dec. 27, 1708.

grounds for accepting their judgment; if the argument of authority is used merely to reënforce strong evidence of other sorts, it is enough to name distinguished specialists who support the view you advocate.

As yet we have comparatively little use for the argument of authority; but even later, when we are depending less on our own experience, the argument of authority should ordinarily not be the sole support of an important proposition.

Not only is it sometimes well to add to the argument of probable cause or reason, the argument of analogy, and to that the argument of example, and to that the argument of authority, it is also effective to multiply each of these arguments — to give several reasons, more than one comparison, a convincing number of examples, an imposing array of authorities.

Let us consider the development of a possible sub-proposition III under the proposition, The pleasures of moderate poverty are greater than the pleasures of wealth.

III. Treats give the moderately poor more pleasure than the rich, for

    A. It is natural that this should be so, for

        1. The treats of the poor are in themselves better suited to give pleasure, for

            a. They are chosen with greater care (evidence ?).

      b. They are chosen with greater sincerity (evidence ?).

  2. The moderately poor are themselves in better condition to derive pleasure from a treat, for (evidence ?).

  3. It is in accord with a universal human tendency, for

      a. The cobbler's children go without shoes.

      b. The hunter cares not for easy game.

      c. The candy maker does not relish sweets.

B. Experience shows that they do, for

  1. When my means were more limited I took greater pleasure in a play.

  2. I took greater pleasure in a trip.

  3. I took greater pleasure in a gift.

  4. I took greater pleasure in a purchase, etc.

C. Others testify that it is so, for

  1. Mrs. A, who was poor in her girlhood and is now rich, says that it is so.

  2. Mrs. B, who was rich in her girlhood and is now poor, says it is true, etc.

In thus piling up evidence to prove a proposition the student should bear in mind that his object is emphasis, and he should take care not to use this device to such excess as to defeat his end. It is advisable to omit questionable or weak evidence; it is often advisable to omit even evidence that is strong. In selecting evidence with a view to emphasis, the value of suggestiveness should not be lost sight of. One or two illustrations or examples that appeal to the reader's experience and set him to calling up evidence on your side out of his own past will do more to convince him than a large number of most conscientiously elaborated instances presented by you. The more varied the evidence the more certain may you be of gaining the interested collaboration of many of your readers.

EXERCISES

1. Give the proposition to be proved in each of the following selections; classify the argument and tell in what respect it is weak or strong: —

a. "Is it so bad, then, to be misunderstood? Pythagoras was misunderstood, and Socrates, and Jesus, and Luther, and Copernicus, and Galileo, and Newton, and every pure and wise spirit that ever took flesh. To be great is to be misunderstood." — EMERSON : *Self-reliance.*

b. "If life is not always poetical, it is at least metrical. Periodicity rules over the mental experience of man, according to the path of the orbit of his thoughts. Distances are not gauged, ellipses not measured, velocities not ascertained, times not known. Nevertheless, the recurrence is sure. What the mind suffered last week, or last year, it does not suffer now, but it will suffer again next week or next year. Happiness is not a matter of events; it depends upon the tides of the mind.   Disease is metrical, closing in at shorter and shorter periods towards death, sweeping abroad at longer and longer intervals towards recovery.   Sorrow for one cause was intolerable yesterday, and will be intolerable to-morrow ; to-day it is easy to bear, but the cause has not passed.   Even the burden of a spiritual distress unsolved is bound to leave the heart to a temporary peace : and re-morse itself does not remain — it returns.   Gayety takes us by a dear surprise." — ALICE MEYNELL : *The Rhythm of Life.*

c. " I believe that natural history has lost much by the vague general treatment that is so common — what satisfac-tion would be derived from a ten-page sketch of the habits and customs of man?   How much more profitable it would be to devote that space to the life of some one great man.   This is the principle I have endeavored to apply to my animals.   The real personality of the individual and his view of life are my theme, rather than the ways of the race in general, as viewed by a casual and hostile human eye." — ERNEST THOMPSON SETON : *Wild Animals I Have Known.*

d. " Besides — Grotius and Lauterbach, and Puffendorff, and Titius, and many wise men beside, who have considered the matter properly, have determined, that the property of a country can not be acquired by hunting, cutting wood, or drawing water in it — nothing but precise demarcation of limits, and the intention of cultivation, can establish the possession.   Now as the savages [Indians] (probably from never having read the authors above quoted) had never com-plied with any of these necessary forms, it plainly follows that they had no right to the soil." — IRVING : *Knicker-bocker History of New York.*

e. " The Mahometans regard their Koran with a reverence

which few Christians pay even to their Bible.   It is admitted everywhere as the standard of all law and all practice ; the thing to be gone upon in speculation and life : the message sent direct out of Heaven, which this Earth has to conform to, and walk by, the thing to be read.   Their Judges decide by it ; all Moslems are bound to study it, seek in it for the light of their life.   They have mosques where it is all read daily ; thirty relays of priests take it up in succession, get through the whole each day.   There, for twelve hundred years, has the voice of this Book, at all moments, kept sounding through the ears and the hearts of so many men." — CARLYLE : *Heroes and Hero-worship.*

f.   " ' But it is so charming to swim on the water ! ' said the Duckling, ' so refreshing to let it close above one's head, and to dive down to the bottom.'

" ' Yes, that must be a mighty pleasure, truly,' quoth the Hen.   ' I fancy you must have gone crazy.   Ask the Cat about it — he's the cleverest animal I know — ask him if he likes to swim on the water, or to dive down.   I won't speak about myself.   Ask our mistress, the old woman ; no one in the world is cleverer than she.   Do you think she has any desire to swim, and to let the water close above her head ? ' " — ANDERSEN : *The Ugly Duckling.*

g.   " Cæsar had his Brutus, Charles I his Cromwell, and George III — may profit by their example." — PATRICK HENRY.

h.   "The candles sputtered, and the hot fat fell on the shavings below.   ' Dangerous way of lighting a room full of shavings,' said some one.   The landlord looked up at the swinging candelabra and laughed.   ' Tried it pretty often,' he said.   ' Never burned a house down yet.' " — H. H. JACKSON.

i.   "The murderers *did* escape from one of these windows. This being so, they could not have refastened the sashes from the inside, as they were found fastened. . . . Yet the sashes *were* fastened. They *must*, then, have the power of fastening themselves. There was no escape from this conclusion. I stepped to the unobstructed casement, withdrew the nail with some difficulty, and attempted to raise the sash. It resisted all my efforts as I had anticipated. A concealed spring must, I now knew, exist; and this corroboration of my idea convinced me that my premises, at least, were correct, however mysterious still appeared the circumstances attending the nails. A careful search soon brought to light the hidden spring. I pressed it, and, satisfied with the discovery, forbore to upraise the sash.

"I now replaced the nail and regarded it attentively. A person passing out through the window might have reclosed it, and the spring would have caught; but the nail could not have been replaced. The conclusion was plain, and again narrowed in the field of my investigations. The assassins *must* have escaped through the other window. Supposing, then, the springs upon each sash to be the same, as was probable, there *must* be found a difference between the nails, or at least between the modes of their fixture. Getting upon the sacking of the bedstead, I looked over the head-board minutely at the second casement. Passing my hand down behind the board, I readily discovered and pressed the spring, which was, as I had supposed, identical in character with its neighbor. I now looked at the nail. It was as stout as the other, and apparently fitted in the same manner, driven in nearly up to the head. . . . It had, I say, in every respect the appearance of its fellow in the other window; but this fact was an absolute nullity, conclusive as it might seem to be, when compared with the consideration that here, at this point, terminated the clue. 'There *must* be something wrong,' I said, 'about the nail.' I touched it, and the head, with about a quarter of an inch of the shank, came off in my fingers. The rest of the shank was in the gimlet-hole, where it had been broken off. The fracture was an old one (for its edges were incrusted with rust), and had apparently been accomplished by the blow of a hammer, which had partially imbedded, in the top of the bottom sash, the head portion of the nail. I now carefully replaced this head portion in the indentation whence I had taken it, and the resemblance to a perfect nail was complete — the fissure was invisible. Pressing the spring, I gently raised the sash for a few inches; the head went up with it, remaining firm in its bed. I closed the window, and the semblance of the whole nail was again perfect.

" The riddle, so far, was now unriddled. The assassin had escaped through the window which looked upon the bed. Dropping of its own accord upon his exit (or perhaps purposely closed), it had become fastened by the spring; and it was the retention of this spring which had been mistaken by the police for that of the nail, — further inquiry being thus considered unnecessary." — POE : *The Murders in the Rue Morgue.*

j. " There was once a little animal,
No bigger than a fox,
And on five toes he scampered
Over Tertiary rocks.
They called him Eohippus,
And they called him very small,
And they thought him of no value —
When they thought of him at all;

*　　*　　*　　*　　*

" Said the little Eohippus,
   ' I am going to be a horse !
And on my middle finger nails
   To run my earthly course !
I'm going to have a flowing tail !
   I'm going to have a mane !
I'm going to stand fourteen hands high
   On the psychozoic plain ! '

" The Coryphodon was horrified,
   The Dinoceras was shocked ;
And they chased young Eohippus,
   But he skipped away and mocked.
Then they laughed enormous laughter,
   And they groaned enormous groans,
And they bade young Eohippus
   Go view his father's bones.
Said they, ' You always were as small
   And mean as now we see,
And that's conclusive evidence
   That you're always going to be.
What ! be a great, tall, handsome beast
   With hoofs to gallop on ?
Why ! you'd have to change your nature ! '
   Said the Loxolophodon.
They considered him disposed of,
   And retired with gait serene ;
That was the way they argued
   In ' the early Eocene.' "
      — C. P. Stetson : *In This Our World.*

k. " ' But we shall live to see the day, I trust,' went on the
artist, ' when no man shall build his house for posterity.   Why

should he? He might just as reasonably order a durable suit of clothes, — leather, or gutta-percha, or whatever else lasts longest, — so that his great-grandchildren should have the benefit of them, and cut precisely the same figure in the world that he himself does.' " — HAWTHORNE : *The House of the Seven Gables.*

l. "*Fal.* What is the gross sum that I owe thee?

"*Host.* Marry, if thou wert an honest man, thyself and the money too. Thou didst swear to me upon a parcel-gilt goblet, sitting in my Dolphin-chamber, at the round table, by a sea-coal fire, upon Wednesday in Wheeson week, when the prince broke thy head for liking his father to a singing-man of Windsor, thou didst swear to me then, as I was washing thy wound, to marry me and make me my lady thy wife. Canst thou deny it? Did not goodwife Keech, the butcher's wife, come in then and call me gossip Quickly? coming in to borrow a mess of vinegar ; telling us she had a good dish of prawns ; whereby thou didst desire to eat some ; whereby I told thee they were ill for a green wound? And didst thou not, when she was gone downstairs, desire me to be no more so familiarity with such poor people; saying that ere long they should call me madam? And didst thou not kiss me and bid me fetch thee thirty shillings? I put thee now to thy book-oath : deny it, if thou canst."

— SHAKESPEARE : 2 *King Henry IV.*

2. In the following passage, what kinds of evidence are in conflict and which seems to you the more convincing?

" ' I'm a very poor man, sir.'

" ' I am sorry to hear it, Mr. Barkis.'

" ' A very poor man, indeed I am,' said Mr. Barkis.

" Here his right hand came slowly and feebly from under the bedclothes, and with a purposeless, uncertain grasp took hold of a stick which was loosely tied to the side of the bed. After some poking about with this instrument, in the course of which his face assumed a variety of distracted expressions, Mr. Barkis poked it against a box, an end of which had been visible to me all the time. Then his face became composed.

"'Old clothes,' said Mr. Barkis.

"'Oh!' said I.

"'I wish it was money, sir,' said Mr. Barkis.

"'I wish it was, indeed,' said I.

"'But it *ain't*,' said Mr. Barkis, opening both his eyes as wide as he possibly could." — DICKENS : *David Copperfield*.

3. What is the proposition to be proved in the following excerpt and what kinds of evidence are used to prove it ? Put material in form of a brief.

"Where, as is often the case on the sea-board or in the glaciated districts of the interior of this country, the trench of the roadway is bottomed in soft sand, some hardening of the surface is necessary, else the roller will churn the sand and broken stone together, until the mixture, which has no value whatever in the road structure, has absorbed, it may be, half of the materials reckoned on for the hardened way. To hold the stone and the sand apart it has been the usual practice to cover the sand with a layer of pebbles of conveniently large size before the bottom layer of broken stone was laid down. This is an expedient which is often costly and sometimes impracticable from lack of fit materials. An experimental inquiry into the conditions of the movement of sand under pressure led to the conclusion that an arrangement which would prevent the sand from mingling with the stones, for the brief time required for the passage of the roller in its first traverses over the road, would attain the desired end. It is not at all needful that the partition should be enduring, for as soon as the lower layer of stones has been forced into contact, and has become bound together, there is no further danger of the mingling of the bits with the sand; thus the speedy decay of the fabric is a matter of no consequence. As the result of careful tests made by Mr. Charles Mills, the chief engineer of the Massachusetts Highway Commission, and with the assistance of Mr. W. P. McClintock, the engineer member of the board, it appeared that ordinary cotton cloth of the cheapest quality, such as goes under the name of cheese-cloth, if spread upon the sand after the road is shaped to receive the broken stone, will serve to keep the stone and sand from churning together. This method was carefully tried in macadamizing the state road between Cottage City and Edgartown, Massachusetts. The cloth was spread in strips lengthwise of the way; the stone for the bottom layer was shoveled from the sides upon it with no unusual care. When the roller came to be used it was found that the stone acted essentially as if it was on an ordinary firm foundation; it at once united with the usual number of passages of the roller over it. At the present price of cotton, cheese-cloth can be had in large quantities at a cost of about three cents per square yard on the road. This for a hardened way fifteen feet in width amounts to about seven hundred and fifty dollars per mile, which is often much less than the cost of any other effective means of attaining the object, and may be less than one third that due to the loss of the broken stone which would occur if it were allowed to come directly in contact with the sand. A section through such a " petti-coat road," as it has been termed, shows that the stones do not tear through the cloth. It is indeed probable that material of even slighter texture and of much less cost would serve. Various kinds of strong paper were tried but found worthless." — N. S. SHALER : *American Highways*.

4. Bring to class a good example from literature of *a priori* reasoning, *a posteriori* reasoning, the argument of analogy, the argument of authority.

5. Reduce to brief form the following argument and expand the derived brief : —

" Here, on the other hand, the women are the real supporters of the ideal endeavors : in not a few fields, their influence is the decisive one; in all fields, this influence is felt, and the whole system tends ever more and more to push the men out and the women in. Theatre managers claim that eighty-five per cent of their patrons are women. No one can doubt that the same percentage would hold for those who attend art exhibitions, and even for those who read magazines and literary works in general. And we might as well continue with the same arbitrary figure : can we deny that there are about eighty-five per cent of women among those who attend public lectures, or who go to concerts, among those who look after public charities and the work of the churches ? I do not remember ever to have been in a German art exhibition where at least half of those present were not men, but I do remember art exhibitions in Boston, New York, and Chicago where, according to my actual count, the men in the hall were less than five per cent of those present. As a matter of course, the patron determines the direction which the development will take. As the political reader is more responsible for the yellow press than is the editor, so all the non-political functions of public life must slowly take, under these conditions, the stamp of the feminine taste and type, which must have again the further effect of repelling man from it more and more. The result is an effemination of the higher culture." — MUNSTERBERG : *American Traits*.

REFUTATION

So far we have considered only the building up of an argument, but when one argues, one must take account of objections that have been expressed or that are likely to arise in the reader's or hearer's mind, and tear down such counter arguments. The overthrow of opposing arguments is called refutation.

It is not always necessary to overthrow all opposing arguments. It is conceivable that, conceding some contentions against your view to have weight, the argument you can make to support a theory, though not perfect, is still strong enough to convince you. Your audience is probably as open to conviction as you are. Certainly the frank admission of a doubt would count less against your cause with any intelligent hearer than a specious argument or a "bluff."

Indeed it must often be the case that a true searcher after truth will communicate to others his hypothesis for the very reason that it has a flaw in it. He will wish to make clear his reasoning so far as he has gone in order to make others interested in working out the unsolved point. The flaw he makes the *raison d'être* for the argument. It is said that it was through explaining to Mrs. Greene the imperfection of his cotton gin that Whitney got the suggestion for the brushes that made it effective. We should not ignore nor pretend to overthrow objections that we can not refute.

Not only should we attempt to refute only what we can honestly refute; it is not necessary always to refute all that we can refute. The strong debater will not be betrayed into a vain display of cleverness in uncovering the fallacies of his opponent if they are unimportant; he will resist the temptation to hold his opponent up to scorn by riddling his argument unnecessarily. If he is actuated by an impersonal desire to prove his proposition, he will select for refutation only those points which he can honestly refute, and of those only the ones that, unrefuted, will seriously impair the validity of his argument.

In studying how to build up an argument we make the best possible preparation for refutation. If we understand the difficulties and pitfalls in the process of constructing an argument, we know where to look for the weak points in an antagonist's argument; on the other hand, all that we learn about detecting fallacies in the arguments of our opponents should help us guard against their occurrence in our own reasoning.

We have learned in previous chapters that we must

have a care to make the basis of evidence broad enough, that the argument must be based on principles or facts, that there must be sequence in the argument, and that the argument of authority is subject to certain restrictions. It is neglect to conform with these requirements that gives rise to fallacies.

In the first place, see that the argument rests on a broad enough base. Is the implied middle term accurate, and the implied major premise in consequence tenable? Is there no illicit assumption? This is one of the most common errors. The youth who came to my door and urged, "You should subscribe for this paper, for I am trying to earn my way through college and your subscription will help me along," made this error. Vainly he proved that he was a college student and intended to use the money for his education; vainly he proved that my subscription would help him pay his expenses; vainly he proved the laudability of his aim, so long as he took for granted my approval of his method. In testing an argument discover the implied major premise and see if it is tenable.

This error often results from the use in the brief of compound or complex propositions and the proof of the last member only. The following is a case in point :—

We should have an endowed theatre, for
It would abolish the "long run," which is one of the objectionable features of the present system, for

The long run tends to produce mechanical acting, for, etc.

The writer in such a case proceeds to establish beyond question the fact that the "long run" is objectionable and counts his work done, forgetting that he has not proved the main point, that the new system will obviate the difficulty. This is a frequent blunder. It is often more glaring, as : —

It would abolish the long run which is fatal to good acting and which now prevails, for

The long run is now customary when a company is making a long stay in one city, for (evidence)

The long run is now the custom when a company is touring the country, for, etc.

Here the writer ignores both the proposition that the endowment will work a change, and the proposition that the long run is objectionable.

In the second place, one should see that the proof rests on facts. Facts offered to prove a point are sometimes in themselves contradictory. A student asserted in a brief that 54 per cent of the voters in Massachusetts were native born and 84 per cent of the voters in Massachusetts were foreign born. As 100 per cent represents all the voters in Massachusetts, it was not necessary to consult statistics to prove these figures erroneous. The student who stated that of 59,250 prisoners one in every 938 was native born and one in every 518 was foreign born, provoked the spontaneous inquiry, "Pray, what are the rest?"

Common sense applied is often all that is needed to show that a statement can not be true.   The claim of a student arguing about orphan asylums, that two hundred and fifty out of every thousand persons in New York State were homeless children, would not be credited by any one who stopped to think that that would mean about a third of the juvenile population of the state, if we allow one fourth of the inhabitants of the state to be adults, and that to house so many children, orphan asylums must be as numerous as schoolhouses.

It is sometimes possible to point out that the evidence offered to support one proposition disproves another, as in the following case :—

" *Towns.* Forsooth, a blind man at Saint Alban's shrine,
Within this half-hour, hath received his sight ;
A man that ne'er saw in his life before.

　*　　　*　　　*　　　*　　　*　　　*　　　*

Glou. Let me see thine eyes : wink now : now open them :
In my opinion yet thou see'st not well.
　　Simpcox. Yes, master, clear as day, I thank God and
　　　　Saint Alban.
　　Glou. Say'st thou me so?   What color is this cloak of ?
　　Simp. Red, master ; red as blood.
　　Glou. Why, that's well said.   What color is my gown of ?
　　Simp. Black, forsooth : coal-black as jet.
　　King. Why, then, thou know'st what color jet is of ?

Suff. And yet, I think, jet did he never see.

Glou. But cloaks and gowns, before this day, a many.

Wife. Never, before this day, in all his life.

Glou. Tell me, sirrah, what's my name?

Simp. Alas, master, I know not.

Glou. What's his name?

Simp. I know not.

Glou. Nor his?

Simp. No, indeed, master.

Glou. What's thine own name?

Simp. Saunder Simpcox, an if it please you, master.

Glou. Then, Saunder, sit there, the lyingest knave in Christendom. If thou hadst been born blind, thou mightst as well have known all our names as thus to name the several colors we do wear. Sight may distinguish of colors; but suddenly to nominate them all, it is impossible." — SHAKESPEARE: 2 *King Henry VI.*

Facts in themselves true may be shown to be misleading by the revelation of suppressed facts. The man who proved his excellent marksmanship by showing a bullet hole in the center of a small target chalked on a barn door, and proved that he shot from an old fowling piece one hundred yards away to make the center hole, had a good case till some one explained that the target was chalked after the bullet was fired. This is more strictly speaking, however, a fallacy of the first class, where the unwarranted assumption is made that the target was there when the bullet hole was made.

If either premise is overthrown, the conclusion is

invalidated.   The following is a good illustration of refutation by overthrowing both the major and the minor premises in the implied syllogism : —

All reformatory measures that would change this govern-ment to a democracy are measures which should not be enacted.

This is a reformatory measure that would change this government to a democracy.

This is a measure that should not be enacted.

" My honorable friend, the member for the University of Oxford, tells us, that if we pass this law, England will soon be a republic.   The reformed House of Commons will, ac-cording to him, before it has sat ten years, depose the king and expel the Lords from their House.   Sir, if my honorable friend could prove this, he would have succeeded in bring-ing an argument for democracy infinitely stronger than any that is to be found in the works of Paine.   My honorable friend's proposition is in fact this : that our monarchical and aristocratical institutions have no hold on the public mind of England ; that these institutions are regarded with aver-sion by a decided majority of the middle class.   This, Sir, I say, is plainly deducible from his proposition ; for he tells us that the representatives of the middle class will inevitably abolish royalty and nobility within ten years ; and there is surely no reason to think that the representatives of the mid-dle class will be more inclined to a democratic revolution than their constituents.   Now, Sir, if I were convinced that the great body of the middle class in England look with aversion on monarchy and aristocracy, I should be forced, much against my will, to come to this conclusion, that mo-narchical and aristocratical institutions are unsuited to my country. Monarchy and aristocracy, valuable and useful as I think them, are still valuable and useful as means and not as ends. The end of government is the happiness of the people; and I do not conceive that, in a country like this, the happiness of the people can be promoted by a form of government in which the middle classes place no confidence, and which exists only because the middle classes have no organ by which to make their sentiments known. But, Sir, I am fully convinced that the middle classes sincerely wish to uphold the royal prerogatives and the constitutional rights of the peers. What facts does my honorable friend produce in support of his opinion? One fact only, and that a fact which has absolutely nothing to do with the question. The effect of this reform, he tells us, would be to make the House of Commons all powerful. It was all powerful once before, in the beginning of 1649. Then it cut off the head of the king, and abolished the House of Peers. Therefore, if it again has the supreme power, it will act in the same manner. Now, Sir, it was not the House of Commons that cut off the head of Charles the First; nor was the House of Commons then all powerful. It had been greatly reduced in numbers by successive expulsions. It was under the absolute dominion of the army. A majority of the House was willing to take the terms offered by the king. The soldiers turned out the majority; and the minority, not a sixth part of the whole House, passed those votes of which my honorable friend speaks, votes of which the middle classes disapproved then, and of which they disapprove still." — MACAULAY : *On the Reform Bill*, March 2, 1831.

Where the truth of a proposition is upheld by the argument of authority it may be overthrown in various ways : the citation of the authority's views may be shown to be wrong ; the passage or utterance itself may be shown to be misquoted or quoted out of context in such a way as to make it liable to misinterpretation. This is done by citing this expression of opinion correctly, or by citing other contradictory expressions of opinion. The authority himself may be attacked as incompetent or prejudiced. Or opposed authorities of greater weight may be cited.

To the demand for evidence the arguer may answer, " Here are facts enough — I offer you indisputable facts." If what he says is true and still the proposition is not proved, it rests with you to show that through some wrench or twist in the reasoning the facts do not support the proposition ; it does not rest upon them.

This may happen when a word is used in a double sense. The following extract from a brief is an example : —

> Labor unions do not protect their members from arbitrary dismissals, for
> 1. Orders come without warning from the officers of the union to stop work, for
>   a. This was the case in the x strike, etc.

However strong the proof that strikes have been called without warning, the statement that the union does not protect the laborer from arbitrary " dismissal," in the sense in which it pretends to protect him, is not proved.

The treacherous complex proposition may be responsible for a departure from the main line of argument. The student mistakes what is accidental for what is essential. Suppose the student arguing on the pleasures of poverty had said instead of "Mrs. B, who was rich and is now poor, testifies to this, for She says," etc., "This is the testimony of Mrs. B, who was rich and is now poor, for," and had gone on to give evidence of her former wealth and her present poverty : he would have given facts, but they would not be facts to sustain the main line of argument ; they would rather be a dangling incumbrance.

The untrained disputant is easily lured from the main argument to account for a general tendency that he has cited as evidence. Thus, instead of giving facts to prove the " long run " prevalent, the student theorizes : —

The long run is prevalent, for
1. It is easier for the actor, for
   a. There is less labor in learning parts.
2. The actor wants what is easy, for
   (an argument to prove that man is lazy).
3. It is cheaper for the manager, for, etc.
4. And the manager wants what is cheap, for
   (an argument to prove that man is eager for gain).

The irrelevancy of such reasoning is easily appreciated when attention is called to it, but a surprising amount of it can pass muster. The listener is aware that something is being proved and he blames himself that he can not follow.

Less common but more awkward even than this arguing aside from the issue is the reasoning in a circle. This happens where the proposition to be proved is used as evidence to support itself: *Nicholas Nickleby* is a better story than *Oliver Twist*, for they were written at the same time, and Dickens was more interested in the former, as is shown by its greater strength.

The justice of Christ's teachings has been called into question because of the Parable of the Vineyard, but the teaching of this parable must be just, since it was spoken by one who taught only what was just and right.

One who gives a general statement to prove a specific case and then tries to prove the general statement by specific cases, whether or not he gives the particular case he started to prove, is virtually committing this fallacy. Instead of arguing actors are lazy, for all men are lazy, for lawyers are lazy, and merchants are lazy, and ditch diggers are lazy, and proving each of these classes to be lazy, it is obvious that it would be more convincing and more possible to prove the class in question lazy by the process to be applied to the several classes.

The practice of massing the refutation at the beginning or the end of the brief is ordinarily ineffective. In general it seems better to scatter the refutation through the brief, considering the objections that may be raised against a proposition in close connection with the positive proof of that proposition.

The objection should be stated in the brief, and its statement should be followed by the refutation introduced by " yet." " Yet," it should be noticed, is a coördinate conjunction, and the refutation must never be numbered as if it were inferior in rank to the point it refutes. The accepted form is as follows : —

II. He is not truthful, for
    A. Although he told the truth in the case referred
       to,
    A^1. Yet, that does not prove him honest, for
        1. It was to his advantage to tell the truth, for
          a. He was sure the truth would be dis-
            covered, etc.

If the objections are strong ones and are known to preoccupy the hearer's mind, it is best, as a rule, to demolish them before presenting your positive argument. This is, however, not an absolute rule. If you have a convincing and captivating argument for a point, you may address it at once even to the prejudiced hearer, trusting it to make him the more willing to surrender his own views when you come to

assail them.   If the objections are of such a nature
that the audience has to be helped to them by the
speaker, that is, if the speaker is guarding against
possible antagonistic after-thoughts, rather than bat-
tering down firmly intrenched views, it is not best to
begin with the statement of objections and the refutation of them.   This holds true for great or small sections of the brief.

EXERCISES

1. How does the artist refute Nello's objection?   What
is the major premise of each ?

" ' Young man, I am painting a picture of Sinon deceiving
old Priam, and I should be glad of your face for my Sinon,
if you'd give me a sitting.'

" Tito Melema started and looked round with a pale
astonishment in his face, as if at a sudden accusation ; but
Nello left him no time to feel at a loss for an answer : ' Piero,'
said the barber, ' thou art the most extraordinary compound
of humors and fancies ever packed into a human skin.
What trick wilt thou play with the fine visage of this young
scholar to make it suit thy traitor?   Ask him rather to turn
his eyes upward, and thou mayst make a Saint Sebastian of
him that will draw troops of devout women ; or, if thou art
in a classical vein, put myrtle about his curls and make him
a young Bacchus, or say rather a Phœbus Apollo, for his
face is as warm and as bright as a summer morning ; it made
me his friend in the space of a *credo*.'

" ' Aye, Nello,' said the painter, speaking with abrupt
pauses, ' and if thy tongue can leave off its everlasting
chirping long enough for thy understanding to consider the

matter, thou mayst see that thou hast just shown the reason why the face of Messer will suit my traitor. A perfect traitor should have a face which vice can write no marks on — lips that will lie with a dimpled smile — eyes of such agate-like brightness and depth that no infamy can dull them — cheeks that will rise from a murder and not look haggard. I say not this young man is a traitor; I mean, he has the face that would make him the more perfect traitor, if he had the heart of one, which is saying neither more nor less than that he has a beautiful face, informed with rich young blood, that will be nourished enough by food, and keep its color without much help of virtue.'" — GEORGE ELIOT : *Romola*.

Would Tito's discomfiture at the artist's request indicate that he is the "ideal traitor"?

2. In the following passage one hypothesis is offered to undermine another. Which is more convincing? What is the major premise of the city editor? Of Gallegher?

" ' I shouldn't be surprised to meet him out walking, right here in Philadelphia,' said one of the staff. ' He'll be disguised, of course, but you could always tell him by the absence of the trigger finger on his right hand. It's missing, you know ; shot off when he was a boy.'

" ' You want to look for a man dressed like a tough,' said the city editor; ' for as this fellow is to all appearances a gentleman, he will try to look as little like a gentleman as possible.'

" ' No, he won't,' said Gallegher, with that calm impertinence that made him dear to us. ' He'll dress just like a gentleman. Toughs don't wear gloves, and you see he's got to wear 'em. The first thing he thought of after doing for Burrbank was of that gone finger, and how he was to hide it. He stuffed the finger of that glove with cotton so's to

make it look like a whole finger, and the first time he takes off that glove they've got him — see, and he knows it.'"
— RICHARD HARDING DAVIS : *Gallegher and Other Stories.*

3. In the following fable does the Ant admit the Fly's facts? Why does she question her conclusion?

" An Ant and a Fly one day disputed as to their respective merits. 'Vile creeping insect !' said the Fly to the Ant, ' can you for a moment compare yourself with me? I soar on the wing like a bird. I enter the palaces of kings, and alight on the heads of princes, nay of emperors, and only quit them to adorn the yet more attractive brow of beauty. Besides, I visit the altars of the gods. Not a sacrifice is offered but is first tasted by me. Every feast, too, is open to me. I sit and drink of the best, instead of living for days on two or three grains of corn as you do.' ' All that's very fine,' replied the Ant; ' but listen to me. You boast of your feasting, but you know that your diet is not always so choice, and you are sometimes forced to eat what nothing would induce me to touch. As for alighting on the heads of kings and emperors, you know very well that whether you pitch on the head of an emperor or an ass (and it is as often on the one as the other), you are shaken off from both with impatience. And, then, the " altars of the gods," indeed ! There and everywhere else you are looked upon as nothing but a nuisance. In the winter, too, while I feed at my ease on the fruit of my toil, what more common than to see your friends dying with cold, hunger, and fatigue?'"

4. Write a paragraph of refutation of real or fancied perversion of facts.

5. The following excerpts are from a discussion in Randall's *Life of Jefferson*, concerning the drafting of the Dec-

laration of Independence. The discussion is based on the conflicting evidence of eminent authorities. The passages cited refer directly to the particular statements of the two men on the subject in question. Does there seem to be misquotation of any kind on the part of either disputant? Where? Suggest broader lines of argument for establishing the weight of probability on one side or the other : —

John Adams to Timothy Pickering — 1822.

"The Committee met, discussed the subject, and then appointed Mr. Jefferson and me to make the draft, I suppose because we were the two first on the list. The sub-committee met. Jefferson proposed to me to make the draft. I said, 'I will not.' 'You should do it.' 'Oh! no.' 'Why will you not? You ought to do it.' 'I will not.' 'Why?' 'Reasons enough.' 'What can be your reasons?' 'Reason first — you are a Virginian, and a Virginian ought to appear at the head of this business. Reason second — I am obnoxious, suspected, and unpopular. You are very much otherwise. Reason third — you can write ten times better than I can.' 'Well,' said Jefferson, 'if you are decided, I will do as well as I can.' 'Very well. When you have drawn it up, we will have a meeting.' A meeting we accordingly had, and conned the paper over. . . . I consented to report it, *and do not now remember that I made or suggested a single alteration.* We reported it to the Committee of five. It was read, and *I do not remember that Franklin or Sherman criticised anything.* We were all in haste. Congress was impatient, and the instrument was reported, as I believe, *in Jefferson's handwriting, as he first drew it.*"

Jefferson to Madison — August 30, 1823.

"Mr. Adams's memory has led him into an unquestionable

error. At the age of eighty-eight, and forty-seven years
after the transactions of Independence, this is not wonderful.
Nor should I, at the age of eighty, on the small advantage of
that difference only, venture to oppose my *memory* to his,
were it not supported by written notes, taken by myself at
the moment and on the spot. [After giving the substance of
Mr. Adams's statement, he continues :] Now these details
are quite incorrect. The Committee of five met ; no such
thing as a sub-committee was proposed, but they unani-
mously pressed on myself alone to undertake the draft. I
consented ; I drew it ; but before I reported it to the Committee, I communicated it *separately* to Dr. Franklin
and Mr. Adams, requesting their corrections, because they
were the two members of whose judgments and amendments
I wished most to have the benefit, before presenting it to
the Committee : and you have seen the original paper now
in my hands, *with the corrections of Dr. Franklin and Mr.*
Adams interlined in their own handwritings. Their altera-
tions were two or three only, and merely verbal. I then
wrote a fair copy, reported it to the Committee, and from
them, unaltered, to Congress. This personal communication
and consultation with Mr. Adams he has misremembered
into the actings of a sub-committee."— H. S. RANDALL : *Life*
of Jefferson.

"After mentioning that Mr. Jefferson attributed his grand-
father's error, in the matter just considered, to the 'failing
memory of eighty-eight, the *assumed* age of Mr. Adams at
the time' (a lamentable 'assumption,' as we believe Mr.
Adams lacked two or three months of that age !), Mr. Charles
F. Adams continues : ' Perceiving also the *awkward nature*
of the *charge* made by one — himself — having, at the moment, nearly attained fourscore, Mr. Jefferson *disclaims all*

reliance upon his recollection, and appeals to the unequivocal authority of his notes, made at the time. This seemed conclusive testimony, sufficient to set the matter at rest forever. But if by those notes is to be understood no more than what has since been published under that name in the first volume of his Correspondence, it is clear, on examination, that they present no evidence, excepting that which may be implied *by their affirming nothing in corroboration.'*"
— *Life and Works of John Adams,* quoted by H. S. RANDALL.

Mr. Randall refers to the above as follows : —

"This is a most extraordinary commentary ! *Does* Mr. Jefferson, in the Madison letter, bring or imply any ' *charge* ' against Mr. Adams on the score of *age,* or any other score ? *Does* he treat him otherwise than *kindly* and *respectfully ? Does* he so far base a claim to superior accuracy on his own *juniority,* that it makes a reference to Mr. Adams's age ' *awkward' ? Does* he (in exact conflict with the preceding hypothesis !) ' disclaim *all* reliance on his recollection ' ? And, lastly, *is* it *true* that Mr. Jefferson's contemporaneous ' notes ' ' affirm *nothing* in corroboration ' of his statements in the premises ? "

Mr. Randall has previously quoted Jefferson as saying in his notes : "The Committee desired *me* to do it — it was *accordingly* done."

6. Read the argument given below and make a brief of it, carefully stating objections and their refutation as in the example furnished : —

¹*A.* Although he has gained convenient contrivances, for

---

¹ Note that this is lettered as if it were the first objection ; when the previous paragraph is taken into consideration this proposition will no longer be *A.*

     1. He has a coach and crutches.

     2. He has a Geneva watch and a Greenwich nautical almanac.

     3. He has notebooks.

     4. He has libraries.

     5. He has insurance societies.

A^1. Yet for each material gain he has suffered a corresponding loss, for

     1^1. He has lost the use of his feet and his muscles.

     2^1. He has lost knowledge of the sun and the stars.

     3^1. He has lost his memory in some degree.

     4^1. His wit is overloaded.

     5^1. Accidents are more frequent.

B. Although his theory of life is higher, for

     1. The highest philosophy was stoicism.

     2. Christianity is now established.

B^1. Yet his life does not so well comport with his theory, for

     1^1. All Stoics were Stoics.

     2^1. In Christendom where is there a Christian?

"Society never advances. It recedes as fast on one side as it gains on the other. It undergoes continual changes; it is barbarous, it is civilized, it is christianized, it is rich, it is scientific; but this change is not amelioration. For everything that is given, something is taken. Society acquires new arts and loses old instincts. What a contrast between the well-clad, reading, writing, thinking American, with a watch, a pencil, and a bill of exchange in his pocket, and the naked New Zealander, whose property is a club, a spear, a mat and an undivided twentieth of a shed to sleep under! But compare the health of the two men and you shall see that the white man has lost his aboriginal strength. If the traveller tell us truly, strike the savage with a broad ax, and in a day or two the flesh shall unite and heal as if you struck the blow into soft pitch ; and the same blow shall send the white to his grave.

" The civilized man has built a coach, but has lost the use of his feet. He is supported on crutches, but lacks so much support of muscle. He has a fine Geneva watch, but he fails of the skill to tell the hour by the sun. A Greenwich nautical almanac he has, and so being sure of the information when he wants it, the man in the street does not know a star in the sky. The solstice he does not observe ; the equinox he knows as little ; and the whole bright calendar of the year is without a dial in his mind. His notebooks impair his memory ; his libraries overload his wit ; the insurance office increases the number of accidents ; and it may be a question whether machinery does not incumber ; whether we have not lost by refinement some energy, by a Christianity intrenched in establishments and forms some vigor of wild virtue. For every Stoic was a Stoic ; but in Christendom where is the Christian?

" There is no more deviation in the moral standard than in the standard of height or bulk. No greater men are now than ever were. A singular equality may be observed between the great men of the first and of the last ages ; nor can all the science, art, religion, and philosophy of the nineteenth century avail to educate greater men than Plutarch's heroes, three or four and twenty centuries ago. Not in time is the race progressive. Phocion, Socrates, Anaxagoras, Diogenes, are great men, but they leave no class. He who is really of their class will not be called by their name, but will be his own man, and in his turn the founder of a sect. The arts and inventions of each period are only its costume, and do not invigorate men. The harm of the improved machinery may compensate its good. Hudson and Behring accomplished so much in their fishing-boats, as to astonish Parry and Franklin, whose equipment exhausted the resources of science and art. Galileo, with an opera glass, discovered a more splendid series of celestial phenomena than any one since. Columbus found the New World in an undecked boat. It is curious to see the periodical disuse and perishing of means and machinery, which were introduced with loud laudation a few years or centuries before. The great genius returns to essential man. We reckoned the improvements of the art of war among the triumphs of science, and yet Napoleon conquered Europe by the bivouac, which consisted of falling back on naked valor and disincumbering it of all aids. The Emperor held it impossible to make a perfect army, says Las Casas, 'without abolishing our arms, magazines, commissaries, and carriages, until, in imitation of the Roman custom, the soldier should receive his supply of corn, grind it in his handmill, and bake his bread himself.'

"Society is a wave. The wave moves onward, but the water of which it is composed does not. The same particle does not rise from the valley to the ridge. Its unity is only phenomenal. The persons who make up a nation to-day, next year die, and their experience with them."

— EMERSON : *Self-Reliance.*

7. Explain the order of the refutation in Decius' speech:

"*Cæsar.* The cause is in my will : I will not come ;
That is enough to satisfy the senate,
But for your private satisfaction,
Because I love you, I will let you know :
Calpurnia here, my wife, stays me at home :

She dreamt to-night she saw my statua,
Which, like a fountain with an hundred spouts,
Did run pure blood ; and many lusty Romans
Came smiling, and did bathe their hands in it :
And these does she apply for warnings, and portents,
And evils imminent ; and on her knee
Hath begg'd that I will stay at home to-day.
   Decius. This dream is all amiss interpreted :
It was a vision fair and fortunate :
Your statue spouting blood in many pipes,
In which so many smiling Romans bathed,
Signifies that from you great Rome shall suck
Reviving blood, and that great men shall press
For tinctures, stains, relics and cognizance.
This by Calpurnia's dream is signified.
   Cæsar. And this way have you well expounded it.
   Decius. I have, when you have heard what I can say :
And know it now : the senate have concluded
To give this day a crown to mighty Cæsar.
If you shall send them word you will not come,
Their minds may change.   Besides, it were a mock,
Apt to be render'd, for some one to say,
' Break up the senate till another time,
When Cæsar's wife shall meet with better dreams.'
If Cæsar hide himself, shall they not whisper,
' Lo, Cæsar is afraid ' ? "
— SHAKESPEARE : Julius Cæsar.

8. Write a brief, using the material on plagiarism given on pages 21–25. Give ample refutation of points against your side of the question.

9. Read carefully, then analyze and make a brief of the following excerpt : —

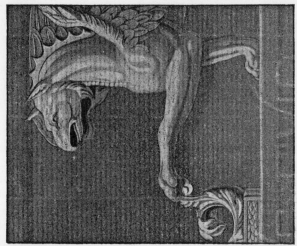

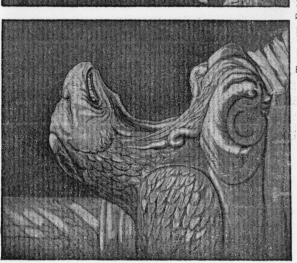

TRUE AND FALSE GRIFFINS.

"On the opposite page, Plate I, I have put, beside each other, a piece of true grotesque, from the Lombard-Gothic, and of false grotesque from classical (Roman) architecture. They are both griffins; the one on the left carries on his back one of the main pillars of the porch in the cathedral of Verona; the one on the right is on the frieze of the temple of Antoninus and Faustina at Rome, much celebrated by Renaissance and bad modern architects.

"In some respects, however, this classical griffin deserves its reputation. It is exceedingly fine in lines of composition, and, I believe (I have not examined the original closely), very exquisite in execution. For these reasons, it is all the better for our purpose. I do not want to compare the worst false grotesque with the best true, but rather, on the contrary, the best false with the simplest true, in order to see how the delicately wrought lie fails in the presence of the rough truth; for rough truth in the present case it is, the Lombard sculpture being altogether untoward and imperfect in execution.

"'Well, but,' the reader says, 'what do you mean by calling *either* of them true? There never were such beasts in the world as either of these?'

"No, never: but the difference is, that the Lombard workman did really see a griffin in his imagination, and carved it from the life, meaning to declare to all ages that he had verily seen with his immortal eyes such a griffin as that; but the classical workman never saw a griffin at all, nor anything else; but put the whole thing together by line and rule.

"'How do you know that?'"

"Very easily. Look at the two, and think over them. You know a griffin is a beast composed of lion and eagle.

The classical workman set himself to fit these together in the most ornamental way possible. He accordingly carves a sufficiently satisfactory lion's body, then attaches very gracefully cut wings to the sides : then, because he cannot get the eagle's head on the broad lion's shoulders, fits the two together by something like a horse's neck (some griffins being wholly composed of a horse and eagle), then, finding the horse's neck look weak and unformidable, he strengthens it by a series of bosses like vertebræ, in front, and by a series of spiny cusps, instead of a mane, on the ridge ; next, not to lose the whole leonine character about the neck, he gives a remnant of the lion's beard, turned into a sort of griffin's whisker, and nicely curled and pointed ; then an eye, probably meant to look grand and abstracted, and therefore neither lion's nor eagle's ; and finally, an eagle's beak, very sufficiently studied from a real one. The whole head being, it seems to him, still somewhat wanting in weight and power, he brings forward the right wing behind it, so as to inclose it with a broad line. . . . The whole griffin, thus gracefully composed, being, nevertheless, when all is done, a very composed griffin, is set to very quiet work, and raising his left foot, to balance his right wing, sets it on the tendril of a flower so lightly as not even to bend it down, though, in order to reach it, his left leg is made half as long again as his right.

" We may be pretty sure, if the carver had ever seen a griffin, he would have reported of him as doing something else than *that* with his feet. Let us see what the Lombardic workman saw him doing.

" Remember, first, the griffin, though part lion and part eagle, has the united *power of both*. He is not merely a bit of lion and a bit of eagle, but whole lion, incorporate with whole eagle. So when we really see one, we may be quite sure we shall not find him wanting in anything necessary to the might either of beast or bird.

"Well, among things essential to the might of a lion, perhaps, on the whole, the most essential are his *teeth*. He could get on pretty well even without his claws, usually striking his prey down with a blow, woundless; but he could by no means get on without his teeth. Accordingly, we see that the real or Lombardic griffin has the carnivorous teeth bare to the root, and the peculiar hanging of the jaw at the back, which marks the flexible and gaping mouth of the devouring tribes.

"Again: among things essential to the might of an eagle, next to his wings (which are of course prominent in both examples) are his *claws*. It is no use his being able to tear anything with his beak, if he can not first hold it in his claws ; he has comparatively no leonine power of striking with his feet, but a magnificent power of grip with them. Accordingly, we see that the real griffin, while his feet are heavy enough to strike like a lion's, has them also extended far enough to give them the eagle's grip with the back claw ; and has, moreover, some of the bird-like wrinkled skin over the whole foot, marking this binding power the more ; and that he has besides verily got something to hold with his feet, other than a flower, of which more presently.

"Now observe, the Lombardic workman did not do all this because he had thought it out, as you and I are doing together ; he never thought a bit about it. He simply saw the beast ; saw it as plainly as you see the writing on this page, and of course could not be wrong in anything he told us of it.

"Well what more does he tell us? Another thing, remember, essential to an eagle is that it should fly *fast*. It is no use its having wings at all if it is to be impeded in the use of them. Now it would be difficult to impede him more thoroughly than by giving him two cocked ears to catch the wind.

"Look, again, at the two beasts. You see the false griffin *has* them so set, and, consequently, as he flew, there would be a continual humming of the wind on each side of his head, and he would have an infallible earache when he got home. But the real griffin has his ears flat to his head, and all the hair of them blown back, even to a point, by his fast flying, and the aperture is downwards, that he may hear anything going on upon the earth, where his prey is. In the false griffin the aperture is upwards.

"Well, what more? As he is made up of the natures of lion and eagle, we may be very certain that a real griffin is, on the whole, fond of eating, and that his throat will look as if he occasionally took rather large pieces, besides being flexible enough to let him bend and stretch his head in every direction as he flies.

"Look, again, at the two beasts, you see the false one has got those bosses upon his neck like vertebræ; which must be infinitely in his way when he is swallowing, and which are evidently inseparable, so that he can not *stretch* his neck any more than a horse. But the real griffin is all loose about the neck, evidently being able to make it almost as much longer as he likes; to stretch and bend it anywhere, and swallow anything, besides having some of the grand strength of the bull's dewlap in it when at rest.

"What more? Having both lion and eagle in him, it is probable that the real griffin will have an infinite look of

repose as well as power of activity.   One of the notablest
things about a lion is his magnificent *indolence*, his look
of utter disdain of trouble when there is no occasion for
it; as, also, one of the notablest things about an eagle is
his look of inevitable vigilance, even when quietest.   Look,
again, at the two beasts.   You see the false griffin is quite
sleepy and dead in the eye, thus contradicting his eagle's
nature, but is putting himself to a great deal of unnecessary trouble with his paws, holding one in a most painful
position merely to touch a flower, and bearing the whole
weight of his body on the other, thus contradicting his
lion's nature.

"But the real griffin is primarily, with his eagle's nature,
wide awake ; evidently quite ready for whatever may happen ; and with his lion's nature, laid all his length on his
belly, prone and ponderous ; his two paws as simply put out
before him as a drowsy puppy's on a drawing-room hearth-
rug ; not but that he has got something to do with them,
worthy of such paws ; but he takes not one whit more
trouble about it than is absolutely necessary.   He has merely
got a poisonous winged dragon to hold, and for such a little
matter as that, he may as well do it lying down and at his
ease, looking out at the same time for any other piece of
work in his way.   He takes the dragon by the middle, one
paw under the wing, another above, gathers him up into
a knot, puts two or three of his claws well into his back,
crashing through the scales of it and wrinkling all the
flesh up from the wound, flattens him down against
the ground, and so lets him do what he likes.   The dragon
tries to bite him, but can only bring his head round far
enough to get hold of his own wing, which he bites in
agony instead ; flapping the griffin's dewlap with it, and

wriggling his tail up against the griffin's throat; the griffin being, as to these minor proceedings, entirely indifferent, sure that the dragon's body cannot drag itself one hair's-breadth off those ghastly claws, and that its head can do no harm but to itself.

"Now observe how in all this, through every separate part and action of the creature, the imagination is *always* right. It evidently *can not* err; it meets every one of our requirements respecting the griffin as simply as if it were gathering up the bones of the real creature out of some ancient rock. It does not itself know or care, any more than the peasant laboring with his spade and axe, what is wanted to meet our theories or fancies. It knows simply what is there, and brings out the positive creature, errorless, unquestionable. So it is throughout art, and in all that the imagination does; if anything be wrong it is not the imagination's fault, but some inferior faculty's, which would have its foolish say in the matter, and meddled with the imagination, and said, the bones ought to be put together tail first, or upside down.

"This however we need not be amazed at, because the very essence of the imagination is already defined to be the seeing to the heart; and it is not therefore wonderful that it should never err; but it is wonderful, on the other hand, how the composing legalism does *nothing else* than err. One would have thought that, by mere chance, in this or the other element of griffin, the griffin-composer might have struck out a truth; that he might have had the luck to set the ears back, or to give some grasp to the claw. But, no; from beginning to end it is evidently impossible for him to be anything but wrong; his whole soul is instinct with lies; no veracity can come within hail of him; to him all regions of right and life are forever closed.

"And another notable point is, that while the imagination receives truth in this simple way, it is all the while receiving statutes of composition also, far more noble than those for the sake of which the truth was lost by the legalist. The ornamental lines in the classical griffin appear at first finer than in the other ; but they only appear so because they are more commonplace and more palpable. The subtlety of the sweeping and rolling curves in the real griffin, the way they waver and change and fold, down the neck, and along the wing, and in and out among the serpent's coils, is incomparably grander, merely as grouping of ornamental line, than anything in the other; nor is it fine as ornamental only, but as massively useful, giving weight of stone enough to answer the entire purpose of pedestal sculpture. Note, especially, the insertion of the three plumes of the dragon's broken wing in the outer angle, just under the large coil of his body ; this filling of the gap being one of the necessities, not of the pedestal block merely, but a means of getting mass and breadth, which all composers desire more or less, but which they seldom so perfectly accomplish.

"So that taking the truth first, the honest imagination gains everything ; it has its griffinism, and grace, and usefulness, all at once : but the false composer, caring for nothing but himself and his rules, loses everything, — griffinism, grace, and all.

"I believe the reader will now sufficiently see how the terms 'true' and 'false' are in the most accurate sense attachable to the opposite branches of what might appear at first, in both cases, the merest wildness of inconsistent reverie. But they are even to be attached, in a deeper sense than that in which we have hitherto used them, to these two compositions.

For the imagination hardly ever works in this intense way, unincumbered by the inferior faculties, unless it be under the influence of some solemn purpose or sentiment. And to all the falseness and all the verity of these two ideal creatures this farther falsehood and verity have yet to be added, that the classical griffin has, at least in this place, no other intent than that of covering a level surface with entertaining form; but the Lombardic griffin is a profound expression of the most passionate symbolism. Under its eagle's wings are two wheels, which mark it as connected, in the mind of him who wrought it, with the living creatures in the vision of Ezekiel: 'When they went, the wheels went by them, and whithersoever the spirit was to go, they went, and the wheels were lifted up over against them, for the spirit of the living creatures was in the wheels.' Thus signed, the winged shape becomes at once one of the acknowledged symbols of the Divine power; and, in its unity of lion and eagle, the workman of the Middle Ages always means to set forth the unity of the human and divine natures. In this unity it bears up the pillars of the Church, set forever as the corner-stone. And the faithful and true imagination beholds it, in this unity, with everlasting vigilance and calm omnipotence, restrain the seed of the serpent crushed upon the earth; leaving the head of it free, only for a time, that it may inflict in its fury profounder destruction upon itself, — in this also full of deep meaning. The Divine power does not slay the evil creature. It wounds and restrains it only. Its final and *deadly* wound is inflicted by itself."

— RUSKIN: *Modern Painters.*

10. Write a complete brief for a long original forensic on the question on which you prepared an introduction to a brief at the close of the work on the introduction.

PRESENTATION OF MATERIAL — THE FORENSIC

THE DEVELOPMENT OF THE FORENSIC

When the brief is completed the problem of general structure is solved. The solution is not necessarily unalterable. If the student in the heat of writing strikes a truer relationship of parts than he discovered in making the brief, he should not spare himself the trouble of readjusting the parts of the brief, even though his instructor has pronounced the brief acceptable. Revision resulting from such afterthoughts will not infrequently be necessary until the student has gained real proficiency in brief drawing. The student should not, however, begin to write with the expectation of making changes in structure. He should have worked over his brief till he feels that he has reached a unified, coherent, and emphatic arrangement of material.

He is then able to concentrate his attention upon the problem of presenting what he has to say with as much force and charm of style as he can command. There is no peculiar law for argumentation of the highest order, — that is, argumentation addressed to an audience whose intelligence is assumed to be equal to the writer's, — no pattern to which all must conform. There is as much room for individuality here as in any field of literature. Given the same brief, we may have as many different developments of it as there are individuals to experiment with it, if only each writes naturally. But very often, at first, the writer feels all his pleasure and power in composition slipping away as he sits down to expand his unyielding brief into a forensic. A statement of propositions and supporting evidence almost repellent in its formality and rigidness is apt to be the result when the student writes for the first time under the dominance of a brief. If he is not pleased with his accomplishment, he should not blame the brief. He should rather bear in mind Phillips Brooks's advice to young preachers. "The true way to get rid of the boniness of a sermon," he told them, "is not by leaving out the skeleton, but by clothing it with flesh."

One who conceives of argumentation as an arid form of discourse in which natural ability to write is at a discount, will scarcely succeed here. It is true that in argumentation a pleasing style without a solid, logical foundation can not make a successful piece of work. It is also true that a good brief developed with fidelity so that the finished forensic shall have the apprentice virtues, — thoroughness, unity, coherence, etc., — even though it has no touch of the true amateur's pleasure in writing, in finding the fit

expression for his idea, may make an acceptable forensic.   But if the brief is a good one, its right development will tax all the skill the writer has.   The
briefs being equally good, the best forensic will be his
who has the most distinguished ability as a writer.
All other forms of discourse — narration, description,
and exposition — are used in the development of an
argument.   That it must here serve a purpose ought
to give point to the story, lucidity to the explanation,
vividness to the description.

You may feel when your brief is finished that all
has been said, and that may be the case. In the
paragraph on society analyzed on page 166 there is
comparatively little development.   But this is not
always the case.   Your brief may say: —

My experience leads me to think treats give the moderately poor more pleasure than the rich, for
> When I was poor I took greater joy in the purchase
> of a luxury.
> When I was poor I took greater joy in the theatre.

See how Charles Lamb makes " Bridget " in her argument on this question develop these propositions : —

" ' Do you remember the brown suit, which you made to
hang upon you, till all your friends cried shame upon you, it
grew so threadbare — and all because of that folio Beau-
mont and Fletcher, which you dragged home late at night
from Barker's in Covent Garden? Do you remember how
we eyed it for weeks before we could make up our minds to
the purchase, and had not come to a determination till it

was near ten o'clock of the Saturday night, when you set off
from Islington, fearing you should be too late — and when
the old bookseller with some grumbling opened his shop, and
by the twinkling taper (for he was setting bedwards) lighted
out the relic from his dusty treasures — and when you lugged
it home, wishing it were twice as cumbersome — and when
you presented it to me — and when we were exploring the
perfectness of it (*collating*, you called it) — and while I was
repairing some of the loose leaves with paste, which your
impatience would not suffer to be left till daybreak — was
there no pleasure in being a poor man? or can those neat
black clothes which you wear now, and are so careful to keep
brushed, since we have become rich and finical — give you
half the honest vanity with which you flaunted it about in
that overworn suit — your old corbeau — for four or five
weeks longer than you should have done, to pacify your
conscience for the mighty sum of fifteen — or sixteen shillings was it? — a great affair we thought it then — which you
had lavished on the old folio.   Now you can afford to buy
any book that pleases you, but I do not see that you ever
bring me home any nice old purchases now.

*   *   *   *   *   *   *

"'You are too proud to see a play anywhere now but in
the pit.   Do you remember where it was we used to sit,
when we saw the Battle of Hexham, and the Surrender of
Calais, and Bannister and Mrs. Bland in the Children in the
Wood — when we squeezed out our shillings apiece to sit
three or four times in a season in the one-shilling gallery —
where you felt all the time that you ought not to have
brought me — and more strongly I felt obligation to you for
having brought me — and the pleasure was the better for a
little shame — and when the curtain drew up, what cared we

for our place in the house, or what mattered it where we were sitting, when our thoughts were with Rosalind in Arden, or with Viola at the Court of Illyria? You used to say that the gallery was the best place of all for enjoying a play socially — that the relish of such exhibitions must be in proportion to the infrequency of going — that the company we met there, not being in general readers of plays, were obliged to attend the more, and did attend, to what was going on, on the stage — because a word lost would have been a chasm, which it was impossible for them to fill up. With such reflections we consoled our pride then, and I appeal to you whether, as a woman, I met generally with less attention and accommodation than I have done since in more expensive situations in the house? The getting in, indeed, and the crowding up those inconvenient staircases, was bad enough, but there was still a law of civility to woman recognized to quite as great an extent as we ever found in the other passages — and how a little difficulty overcome heightened the snug seat and the play, afterwards!'"

— CHARLES LAMB: Old China.

The first proposition is made convincing to the reader by the detailed narration of a signal instance — the purchase of the folio; the second, by an explanation of the compensations that attend a gallery seat in the theatre.

You will notice in the selection from Emerson, already referred to, the tendency to repeat an idea several times: —

"Society never advances. It recedes as fast on one side as it gains on the other. It undergoes continual changes —

but this change is not amelioration. For everything that is given, something is taken. Society acquires new arts, and loses old instincts. Society is a wave," etc.

Fox is said to have declared that to the multitude one argument stated in five different forms is equal to five new arguments. The single statement in the brief should show that the student does not make this error. But in his forensic he may often with profit resort to repetition, either to emphasize or to make clear an idea. It was a habit that Burke did not lose by. Take for example his iteration and reiteration of the idea that it was not what England could, but what she ought to do with reference to the American colonies that was the question of importance : —

"The question with me is, not whether you have a right to render your people miserable, but whether it is not your interest to make them happy. It is not what a lawyer tells me I *may* do, but what humanity, reason and justice tell me I *ought* to do. Is a politic act the worse for being a generous one? Is no concession proper but that which is made from your want of right to keep what you grant? Or does it lessen the grace or dignity of relaxing in the exercise of an odious claim because you have your evidence-room full of titles, and your magazines stuffed with arms to enforce them? What signify all those titles, and all those arms? Of what avail are they, when the reason of the thing tells me that the assertion of my title is the loss of my suit, and that I could do nothing but wound myself by the use of my own weapons?

"Such is steadfastly my opinion of the absolute necessity of keeping up the concord of this empire by a unity of spirit, though in a diversity of operations, that if I were sure the colonists had at their leaving this country sealed a regular compact of servitude, that they had solemnly abjured all the rights of citizens, that they had made a vow to renounce all ideas of liberty for them and their posterity to all generations; yet I should hold myself obliged to conform to the temper I found universally prevalent in my own day, and to govern two million of men, impatient of servitude, on the principles of freedom. I am not determining a point of law; I am restoring tranquillity; and the general character and situation of a people must determine what sort of government is fitted for them. That point nothing else can or ought to determine."—BURKE: *Conciliation with the Colonies.*

There is, of course, always the danger of excess. You must be sure your idea is worth repeating; that it needs explanation and enforcement; and that you repeat it in such wise as to illumine, not darken; to strengthen, not enfeeble.

EXERCISES

1. Use analogy to show that the following assertions may be true: —

a. If a student has little ability for mathematics, it is the more important that he should study the subject.

b. It is fortunate for a strong character like Lincoln to have to contend against hardships.

c. Fair faces are sometimes deceiving.

d. You can put no reliance on a man without principle.

e. That man's exuberance of spirit is too uniform to be genuine.

f. We are often unaware of those influences that have most deeply affected us.

g. Russia needed a good defeat.

h. Some penalty must be paid for every great social reform.

2. Sustain the following propositions by authority : —

a. The sentence, " She looked beautifully," is incorrect. (Cite the usage of good authors, the opinions of grammarians and lexicographers.)

b. Washington's army suffered great hardships while at Valley Forge.

3. Prove the truth of the two propositions just given by presenting reasons.

4. Choose one of the following generalizations and develop it by presenting numerous examples briefly but in a varied and suggestive way. Choose another generalization and give one excellent, well-developed example in proof of it : —

a. Honesty is the best policy.

b. The gods bring thread for a web begun.

c. The deepest natures develop slowly.

d. Familiarity breeds contempt.

e. College education is not necessary to business success.

f. Animal stories have recently been very popular.

g. Most people have some pet economy.

h. The evil that men do lives after them.

i. A little learning is a dangerous thing.

j. A spice of danger attracts.

k. Forbidden fruits are sweetest.

l. Where there's a will there's a way.

m. Dame Fortune is fickle.

5. Tell by what method or methods each of the following bits of argument is developed : —

a. "The most polite age is in danger of being the most vicious.

"It happened at Athens, during a public representation of some play exhibited in honor of the commonwealth, that an old gentleman came too late for a place suitable to his age and quality. Many of the young gentlemen who observed the difficulty and confusion he was in, made signs to him that they would accommodate him if he came where they sat. The good man bustled through the crowd accordingly ; but when he came to the seats to which he was invited, the jest was to sit close and expose him, as he stood out of countenance, to the whole audience. The frolic went round all the Athenian benches. But on those occasions there were also particular places assigned for foreigners. When the good man skulked towards the boxes appointed for the Lacedemonians, that honest people, more virtuous than polite, rose up all, to a man, and with the greatest respect received him among them. The Athenians, being suddenly touched with a sense of the Spartan virtue and their own degeneracy, gave a thunder of applause ; and the old man cried out, 'The Athenians understand what is good, but the Lacedemonians practice it!'" — STEELE : *The Spectator*.

b. "I shall, in parting, allude to one or two traits in Joanna's demeanor on the scaffold, and to one or two in that of the bystanders, which authorize me in questioning an opinion of his [M. Michelet's] upon this martyr's firmness. The reader ought to be reminded that Joanna d'Arc was subjected to an unusually unfair trial of opinion. Any of the elder Christian martyrs had not much to fear of *personal* rancor. The martyr was chiefly regarded as the enemy of Cæsar; at times, also, where any knowledge of the Christian faith and morals existed, with the enmity that arises spontaneously in the worldly against the spiritual. But the martyr, though disloyal, was not supposed to be, therefore, anti-national; and still less was *individually* hateful. What was hated (if anything) belonged to his class, not to himself separately. Now, Joanna, if hated at all, was hated personally, and in Rouen on national grounds. Hence there would be a certainty of calumny arising against *her*, such as would not affect martyrs in general. That being the case, it would follow of necessity that some people would impute to her a willingness to recant. No innocence could escape *that*. Now, had she really testified this willingness on the scaffold, it would have argued nothing at all but the weakness of a genial nature shrinking from the instant approach of torment. And those will often pity that weakness most, who, in their own persons, would yield to it least. Meantime, there never was a calumny uttered that drew less support from the recorded circumstances. It rests upon no *positive* testimony, and it has a weight of contradicting testimony to stem. And yet, strange to say, M. Michelet, who at times seems to admire the Maid of Arc as much as I do, is the one sole writer amongst her *friends* who lends some countenance to this odious slander. His words are that, if she did not utter this word *recant* with her lips, she uttered it in her heart. 'Whether she *said* the word is uncertain; but I affirm that she *thought* it.'

"Now, I affirm that she did not; not in any sense of the word '*thought*' applicable to the case. Here is France calumniating *La Pucelle*: here is England defending her. M. Michelet can only mean that, on *a priori* principles, every woman must be liable to such a weakness: that Joanna was a woman ; *ergo*, that she was liable to such a weakness.   That is, he only supposes her to have uttered the word by an argument which presumes it impossible for anybody to have done otherwise.   I, on the contrary, throw the *onus* of the argument not on presumable tendencies of nature, but on the known facts of that morning's execution, as recorded by multitudes.   What else, I demand, than mere weight of metal, absolute nobility of deportment, broke the vast line of battle then arrayed against her?   What else but her meek, saintly demeanor won from the enemies, that till now had believed her a witch, tears of rapturous admiration?   'Ten thousand men,' says M. Michelet himself, 'ten thousand men wept;' and of these ten thousand the majority were political enemies knitted together by cords of superstition.   What else was it but her constancy, united with her angelic gentleness, that drove the fanatic English soldier — who had sworn to throw a faggot on her scaffold, as *his* tribute of abhorrence, that *did* so, that fulfilled his vow — suddenly to turn away a penitent for life, saying everywhere that he had seen a dove rising upon wings to heaven from the ashes where she had stood? What else drove the executioner to kneel at every shrine for pardon to *his* share in the tragedy?   And if all this were insufficient, then I cite the closing act of her life, as valid on her behalf, were all other testimonies against her.   The executioner had been directed to apply his torch from below.   He did so.   The fiery smoke rose upwards in billowing volumes. A Dominican monk was then standing almost at her side. Wrapped up in his sublime office, he saw not the danger, but still persisted in his prayers.   Even then, when the last enemy was racing up the fiery stairs to seize her, even at that moment did this noblest of girls think only for *him*, the one friend that would not forsake her, and not for herself; bidding him with her last breath to care for his own preservation, but to leave *her* to God.   That girl, whose latest breath ascended in this sublime expression of self-oblivion, did not utter the word *recant* either with her lips or in her heart.   No ; she did not, though one should rise from the dead to swear it."

— DE QUINCEY : *Joan of Arc.*

c. "But now, furthermore, give me leave to ask, whether the way of doing it [stopping the trade in slaves] is this somewhat surprising one, of trying to blockade the Continent of Africa itself, and to watch slave-ships along that extremely extensive and unwholesome coast ?   The enterprise is very gigantic ; and proves hitherto as futile as any enterprise has lately done.   Certain wise men once, before this, set about confining the cuckoo by a big circular wall ; but they could not manage it ! — Watch the coast of Africa?   That is a very long Coast ; good part of the Coast of the terraqueous Globe !   And the living centers of this slave mischief, the live coals that produce all this world-wide smoke, it appears lie simply in two points, Cuba and Brazil, which *are* perfectly accessible and manageable.

*   *   *   *   *   *   *

"Most thinking people, — if hen-stealing prevail to a plainly unendurable extent, will you station police-officers at every hen-roost ; and keep them watching and cruising incessantly to and fro over the Parish, in the unwholesome dark, at enormous expense, with almost no effect?   Or will you not try rather to discover where the fox's den is, and kill the fox !   Which of those two things will you do?   Most thinking people, you know the fox and his den : there he is, — kill him and discharge your cruisers and police-watchers." — CARLYLE : *The Nigger Question.*

d. " It is an undeniable fact that we cannot know anything whatever except as contrasted with something else. The contrast may be bold and sharp, or it may dwindle into a slight discrimination, but it must be there. If the figures on your canvas are indistinguishable from the background, there is surely no picture to be seen. Some element of unlikeness, some germ of antagonism, some chance for discrimination, is essential to every act of knowing. . . . It is not a superficial but a fundamental truth, that if there were no color but red it would be exactly the same thing as if there were no color at all. In a world of unqualified redness, our state of mind with regard to color would be precisely like our state of mind in the present world with regard to the pressure of the atmosphere if we were always to stay in one place. We are always bearing up against the burden of this deep aërial ocean, nearly fifteen pounds upon every square inch of our bodies ; but until we get a chance to discriminate, as by climbing a mountain, we are quite unconscious of this heavy pressure. In the same way, if we knew but one color we should know no color. If our ears were to be filled with one monotonous roar of Niagara, unbroken by alien sounds, the effect upon consciousness would be absolute silence. If our palates had never come in contact with any tasteful thing save sugar, we should know no more of sweetness than of bitterness. If we had never felt physical pain, we could not recognize physical pleasure. For want of the contrasted background its pleasurableness would be nonexistent. And in just the same way it follows that without knowing that which is morally evil we could not possibly recognize that which is morally good. Of these antagonist correlatives, the one is unthinkable in the absence of the other. In a sinless and painless world, human conduct might possess more outward marks of perfection than any saint ever dreamed of; but the moral element would be lacking; the goodness would have no more significance in our conscious life than that load of atmosphere which we are always carrying about with us.

"We are thus brought to a striking conclusion, the essential soundness of which cannot be gainsaid. In a happy world there must be sorrow and pain, and in a moral world the knowledge of evil is indispensable." — FISKE : *The Mystery of Evil.*

e. "It seems that a really great author must admit of translation, and that we have a test of his excellence when he reads to advantage in a foreign language as well as in his own. Then Shakespeare *is* a genius because he can be translated into German, and *not* a genius because he can not be translated into French. Then the multiplication-table is the most gifted of all conceivable compositions, because it loses nothing by translation, and can hardly be said to belong to any one language whatever. Whereas I should rather have conceived that, in proportion as ideas are novel and recondite, they would be difficult to put into words, and that the very fact of their having insinuated themselves into one language would diminish the chance of that happy accident being repeated in another. In the language of savages you can hardly express any idea or act of the intellect at all : is the tongue of the Hottentot or Esquimaux to be made the measure of the genius of Plato, Pindar, Tacitus, St. Jerome, Dante, or Cervantes ?

"Let us recur, I say, to the illustration of the Fine Arts. I suppose you can express ideas in painting which you can not express in sculpture ; and the more an artist is of a painter, the less he is likely to be of a sculptor. The more he commits his genius to the methods and conditions of his own art, the less he will be able to throw himself into the circumstances of another. Is the genius of Fra Angelico, of Francia, or Raffaelle disparaged by the fact that he was able to do that in colors which no man that ever lived, which no angel, could achieve in wood? Each of the Fine Arts has its own subject-matter; from the nature of the case you can do in one what you can not do in another; you can do in painting what you can not do in carving; you can do in oils what you can not do in fresco; you can do in marble what you can not do in ivory; you can do in wax what you can not do in bronze. Then I repeat, applying this to the case of languages, why should not genius be able to do in Greek what it can not do in Latin? and why are its Greek and Latin works defective because they will not turn into English? That genius, of which we are speaking, did not make English; it did not make all languages, present, past, and future; it did not make the laws of *any* language: why is it to be judged of by that in which it had no part, over which it has no control?"— NEWMAN: *Literature*.

THE ARTICULATION OF THE PARTS

In a long forensic that falls naturally into several sections related to the main subject, but more or less independent of each other, it is sometimes difficult to give the effect of unity. The reader is apt to have a fragmentary notion; parts he remembers, but he has only a dim notion of their connection and bearing, no sense of the force of the entire argument. The most important means of making a paper seem unified is, of course, to make it unified, to keep the central idea dominant and develop I, II, III, etc., strictly for the purpose of proving the main proposition, allowing no digressions or surplusage. That is the work of the brief; but even where the relationship exists and is so baldly evident as in the brief, we are glad to have the numbers and letters to point it out. In the forensic, where the argument is not so directly and concisely stated, and where the letters and numbers are not used, some help is needed to make the average reader aware whither the most orderly argument is tending. These aids are the introduction, transitions, and the conclusion.

The introduction may do much toward making clear what was obscure, toward winning a hostile reader to take the writer's point of view, and so on, but its most important function, perhaps, is to give the reader a comprehensive view of the question as a whole, and the bearing of the discussion of the several particular issues in reference to it. This may be done with more or less explicitness and formality. Cardinal Newman closes the introduction to his lectures on the purpose of the university thus :—

"I have then to investigate in the Discourses which follow, those qualities and characteristics of the intellect in which its cultivation issues or rather consists; and with a view of assisting myself in this undertaking, I shall recur to certain questions which have already been touched upon. These questions are three: viz. the relation of intellectual culture, first, to *mere* knowledge ; secondly, to *professional* knowledge ; and thirdly, to *religious* knowledge.   In other words, are *acquirements* and *attainments* the scope of a University Education? or *expertness in particular arts and pursuits?* or *moral and religious proficiency?* or something besides these three?   These questions I shall examine in succession, with the purpose I have mentioned."

With much less formality Stevenson suggests the divisions for his discussion of the difference between the Scotch and the English in *The Foreigner at Home :* —

"England and Scotland differ, indeed, in law, in history, in religion, in education, and in the very look of nature and men's faces, not always widely, but always trenchantly."

The less obvious, more incidental method of pointing the way is better suited to the lighter subject.

Another opportunity to give an impression of totality, to present the parts in relation to the whole, comes at the close of the forensic.   The conclusion is often used for the purpose of summing up what the writer has sought to accomplish by the entire paper : —

"And now I consider I have said enough in proof of the first point, which I undertook to maintain, viz., the claim of Theology to be represented among the Chairs of a University.   I have shown, I think, that exclusiveness really attaches, not to those who support that claim but to those who dispute it.   I have argued in its behalf, first, from the consideration that, whereas it is the very

profession of a University to teach all sciences, on this account it can not exclude Theology without being untrue to
its profession.   Next, I have said that, all sciences being connected together, and having bearings one on another, it is impossible to teach them all thoroughly, unless they all are taken
into account, and Theology among them.   Moreover, I have
insisted on the important influence which Theology in
matter of fact does and must exercise over a great variety of
sciences, completing and correcting them : so that, granting
it to be a real science occupied upon truth, it cannot be
omitted without great prejudice to the teaching of the rest.
And lastly, I have urged that, supposing Theology be not
taught, its province will not simply be neglected, but will be
actually usurped by other sciences, which will teach, without
warrant, conclusions of their own in a subject-matter which
needs its own proper principles for its due formation and
disposition." — NEWMAN : *The Idea of a University.*

So clear and direct a summary is very welcome
at the close of a long, intricate discourse that one
has followed eagerly without stopping to take one's
bearings.   Usually a writer chooses a more subtle but
not less sure method of utilizing the conclusion as a
unifying element.   Instead of reiterating what he has
said he gives his argument some fresh application
that brings out effectively its force and significance.
Such a conclusion is that at the close of Burke's
Bristol speech.   After discussing the several charges
he said : —

"And now, gentlemen, on this serious day, when I come,
as it were, to make up my account with you, let me take

to myself some degree of honest pride on the nature of the charges that are against me. I do not here stand before you accused of venality, or of neglect of duty. It is not said that, in the long period of my service, I have in a single instance sacrificed the slightest of your interests to my ambition, or to my fortune. It is not alleged that, to gratify any anger or revenge of my own or of my party, I have had a share in wronging or oppressing any description of men, or any one man in any description. No! the charges against me are all of one kind: that I have pushed the principles of general justice and benevolence too far, further than a cautious policy would warrant, and further than the opinions of many would go along with me. In every accident which may happen through life — in pain, in sorrow, in depression and distress — I will call to mind this accusation and be comforted."

But it is not only at the beginning and at the end of the argument that it is desirable to have its course indicated. After proving x, y, z, under I, how shall the writer take up II, without an apparent break? By summing up what has been said and relating it to the main idea, the thought is brought back to the right starting point for the second chain of argument. A transitional sentence or paragraph, summing up what has been said and hinting at what is to come, must frequently be introduced as a connecting link between sections of the argument. Such transitions are frequent in the most informal papers; in *The Foreigner at Home*, already referred to, are such transitions as: —

"But it is not alone in scenery and architecture that we count England foreign. The constitution of society, the very pillars of the empire, surprise and even pain us."

In more pretentious and formal discussions such transitions as the following ones taken from Burke's *Speech on Conciliation* are necessary : —

"These, Sir, are my reasons for not entertaining that high opinion of untried force, by which many gentlemen, for whose sentiments in other particulars I have great respect, seem to be so greatly captivated. But there is still behind a third consideration concerning this object, which serves to determine my opinion on the sort of policy which ought to be pursued in the management of America, even more than its population and its commerce : I mean its *temper and character*."

Or, —

"If then, the removal of the causes of this spirit of American liberty be for the greater part, or rather entirely, impracticable ; if the ideas of criminal process be inapplicable, or, if applicable, are in the highest degree inexpedient ; what way yet remains ? No way is open but the third and last, — to comply with the American spirit as necessary ; or, if you please, to submit to it as a necessary evil."

Introductions, transitions, and conclusions should be in a style suited to the style of the paper as a whole. Every student should know how to write the clear, direct introduction, transitions, and conclusion, that belong to the formal paper ; but they would be out of keeping with the style of the rest of his forensic and should be translated into passages that point the way more casually, more incidentally, without drawing so much attention to themselves. Often these aids to coherence are so obvious and rigid that they remind one forcibly of the brief. One is aware of the brief not as an informing bony structure, but as an external visible coat of mail.

Not only in the style but in the phraseology of the introduction, transitions, and conclusions should the student guard against stilted reminders of the brief. He should avoid such phrases as, "the material issues," "the proposition," "refutation"; he should vary the expression for the relationship between proposition and proof, and not eternally use "for"; he should not announce that he "has proved" or is "going to prove."

Less excusable than these faults, and even more serious, is that of introducing into the forensic the jargon of the academic debate. Some students seem to think that such expressions as "we of the affirmative," "the negative," "our contention is," "it is admitted by both sides," etc., are essential to argumentation, and when they sit down to write a forensic it is as if they represented a debating team with an organized opposed force. The style here should be free from affectation, simple, and natural. The brief should be felt throughout as giving strength and symmetry to the forensic, but it should never declare itself.

EXERCISES

1. What are the strong points of the following passage considered as an introduction : —

" As I sit at my work at home, which is at Hammersmith, close to the river, I often hear some of that ruffianism go past the window, of which a good deal has been said in the papers of late, and has been said before at recurring periods. As I hear the yells and shrieks and all the degradation cast on the glorious tongue of Shakespeare and Milton, as I see the brutal reckless faces and figures go past me, it rouses the recklessness and brutality in me also, and fierce wrath takes possession of me, till I remember, as I hope I mostly do, that it was my good luck only of being born respectable and rich, that has put me on this side of the window among delightful books and lovely works of art, and not on the other side, in the empty street, the drink-steeped liquor-shops, the foul and degraded lodgings. I know by my own feelings and desires what these men want, what would have saved them from this lowest depth of savagery : employment which would foster their self-respect and win the praise and sympathy of their fellows, and dwellings which they could come to with pleasure, surroundings which would soothe and elevate them, reasonable labor, reasonable rest. There is only one thing that can give them this — art." — WILLIAM MORRIS.

2. Write a formal conclusion to a forensic for which the foregoing excerpt might serve as an introduction.

3. Organize in the form of a brief the material furnished by the following summary : —

" The pursuit of perfection, then, is the pursuit of sweetness and light. He who works for sweetness and light, works to make reason and the will of God prevail. He who works for machinery, he who works for hatred, works only for confusion. Culture looks beyond machinery; culture hates hatred; culture has one great passion, the passion for sweetness and light. It has one even yet greater ! — the passion for making them *prevail*. It is not satisfied till we *all* come to a perfect man; it knows that the sweetness and light of the few must be imperfect until the raw and unkindled masses of humanity are touched with sweetness and light." — MATTHEW ARNOLD : *Sweetness and Light*.

4. Select from literature a good formal introduction, an informal, persuasive introduction, several good formal transitions, a good formal conclusion, a good informal conclusion.

5. Write a formal introduction and conclusion to the forensic for which you have prepared the brief.

6. Write transitions to connect the various sections of the argument.

7. Rewrite your introduction, your transitions, and your conclusion, making them less stiff and formal and giving them literary quality.

PERSUASION

We have supposed ourselves arguing always to convince an ideal audience, one that is impartial, well informed, critical. With such an audience the strongest argument is most persuasive, and the writer or speaker may lose himself in his argument without thought of those addressed. Since, however, there are few ideal hearers, and since sound argument will not always bring others to accept your views, persuasion, or the suiting the argument to the hearer, is an important element in popular argument. When the orator takes advantage of the ignorance of his hearers to move them with specious reasoning, with a mere show of logic, he is doing an unworthy thing; when, however, he presents a truly logical and convincing discourse in such a way as to overcome prejudice, his achievement is praiseworthy.

At this stage of our work it is best to make a brief with conviction alone in mind, but at the same time we should recognize that persuasion is not less a matter of selection and arrangement than of expression. In the following passage, Mr. Joel Chandler Harris gives a bit of primitive persuasion that accomplishes its end because " Brer Rabbit " knows the one idea that will appeal to " Brer Fox " : —

" ' I don't keer w'at you do wid me, Brer Fox,' sezee, 'so you don't fling me in dat brier-patch. Roas' me, Brer Fox,' sezee, ' but don't fling me in dat brier-patch,' sezee.

" ' Hit's so much trouble fer ter kindle a fier,' sez Brer Fox, sezee, 'dat I speck I'll hatter hang you,' sezee.

" ' Hang me des ez high as you please, Brer Fox,' sez Brer Rabbit, sezee, ' but do fer de Lord's sake don't fling me in dat brier-patch,' sezee.

" ' I ain't got no string,' sez Brer Fox, sezee, ' en now I speck I'll hatter drown you,' sezee.

" ' Drown me des ez deep ez you please, Brer Fox,' sez

Brer Rabbit, sezee, 'but do-don't fling me in dat brier-patch,' sezee.

"'Dey ain't no water nigh,' sez Brer Fox, sezee, 'en now I speck I'll hatter skin you,' sezee.

"'Skin me, Brer Fox,' sez Brer Rabbit, sezee, 'snatch out my eyeballs, t'ar out my years by de roots, en cut off my legs,' sezee, 'but do please, Brer Fox, don't fling me in dat brier-patch,' sezee.

"Co'se Brer Fox wanter hurt Brer Rabbit bad ez he kin, so he cotch 'im by de behime legs en slung 'im right in de middle er de brier-patch.

* * * * * * *

"Brer Rabbit was bleedzed fer ter fling back some er his sass, en he holler out:

"'Bred en bawn in a brier-patch, Brer Fox — bred en bawn in a brier-patch!' en wid dat he skip out des ez lively ez a cricket in de embers." — JOEL CHANDLER HARRIS : *Uncle Remus*.

The order of presentation has much to do with the acceptability of an idea. An audience may by degrees be won to receive with favor ideas that, given at the start, would have roused resistance. Mark Antony's speech over the body of Cæsar furnishes us with an example of this; his excited hearers would scarcely have permitted him to speak had he begun —

"Then I, and you, and all of us fell down,
    Whilst bloody treason flourish'd over us."

or,

"... but were I Brutus,
And Brutus Antony, there were an Antony
Would ruffle up your spirits and put a tongue

In every wound of Cæsar that should move
The stones of Rome to rise and mutiny."
— SHAKESPEARE : *Julius Cæsar*.

When we speak of a persuasive style we usually
mean a style that wins gently and pleasantly ; in a
broader sense, however, a persuasive style is one that
effects the speaker's wish.   Whether it be suave or
brusque, gracious or austere, will depend upon the
audience to be influenced.   There are some with
whom a bluff, rough-and-ready style works wonders,
while a suggestion of the unctuous repels irretriev-
ably.

Whether one depends upon selection, arrangement,
or style, or on all three, to accomplish his purpose,
his art, to succeed, must conceal itself.   We must, like
Antony, give the impression that, " I am no orator,
as Brutus is ; but . . . a plain, blunt man."   Men re-
sent the suggestion of insincerity in a speaker, the
suggestion that they are being led blindfold, to some
goal that they have no desire to reach — wise men,
however, often feel justified in using art to induce
men to listen to what they otherwise might reject.

Ruskin's address called *Work* is an excellent example of this.   The address was prepared to be de-
livered before workingmen.   Ruskin begins as if he
were not in the least a reformer with concern for the
conduct of his hearers, but as if they were all students
of economics interested in social classes, bent on dis-

covering the distinctions that exist among industrious men, "who whether they work or whether they play put their strength into the work and their strength into the game." These he says are mainly four : —

I. Between those who work and those who play.

II. Between those who produce the means of life and those who consume them.

III. Between those who work with the head and those who work with the hand.

IV. Between those who work wisely and those who work foolishly.

The first distinction proves to be mainly a device to bring his hearers to his idea of the distinction between producer and consumer. By his novel nomenclature he rouses curiosity and puts his audience into a receptive state of mind. Had he begun at once with the time-honored "consumer" and "producer," each man would have called up his own long-entertained, possibly half or wholly wrong idea to fit the word, and Ruskin's labor to modify and correct their ideas would have been futile.

We find on reading that the only inevitable distinction is between head workers and hand workers; that the other distinctions are wrong and must pass away, but that there must always be head work and hand work, and that there must always be "rough" men to do the hand work and "gentlemen" to do the gentle work. If all the other distinctions are wrong

and transient, why are they not treated together?
Why is this fundamental distinction slipped in between them? If we think of Ruskin as trying to carry
his audience rather than as trying to give a coherent
and emphatic exegesis of his subject, the question is
easily answered.   It was more persuasive to begin
with a distinction between the classes, that he would
denounce, that he could speak of as one sure to
pass away.   Having shown his hearers his understanding and sympathy, he now dares to tell them
plainly of a distinction that he believes must endure,
taking pains to admit, in order not to lose ground, that
under the present system the head work and the hand
work are not always assigned to those best fitted for
them and that the hand work is not properly rewarded,
but he remains firm on the point that it is not their
business, but the business of the head workers, to rec-
tify the evils.   He has granted that one distinction is
unjust and forced them to admit one to be just — to
recognize their limitations, he now presents a distinction that should not endure, that makes for unhappi-
ness, one that they can help overcome, and proceeds
to give a sermon that each man may take home to his
bosom and business, a sermon which, if given at the
outset, few would have received willingly.

The power to win an audience to care for that
to which they were indifferent, to accept what they
have willed not to accept, is not to be lightly esteemed.

Many covet it; most of us like to watch the process
of persuasion, to note the maneuvers by which the
speaker brings about desired results, to detect the
transparent devices of the teacher who holds the children as in a spell while she "talks down" to them,
the adroitness of the demagogue haranguing a ward
meeting, the subtilities of the employer or the union
leader pacifying a mob of strikers. But let any of
these things be done clumsily, so that the art is
patent to those who should not be aware of it, and
what derision is roused. The effect must be that of
sincerity. It is usually safest really to be sincere.
There are ways of gaining the end without trickery,
without playing upon vanity or weakness. Garfield's
"God reigns, and the government at Washington still
survives" sent the would-be avengers of Lincoln's
death to their homes. The union men assembled in
Faneuil Hall did listen to President Eliot of Harvard
while he told them with unqualified directness what
he thought of the system of "picketing" and the
"closed shop."

Any false emotion in a forensic weakens it. A
forensic may be challenging, belligerent, scornful, —
what not? if the occasion justifies the emotion and
the writer really has it. But even where there is
ample justification for strong feeling, it may be
doubted whether an emotional appeal makes the
deep and lasting impression that does the utterance

of one, not swept off his feet by sudden feeling, but calmly pronouncing a deep-rooted, dispassionate view.

The highest sort of persuasion is that of the man who has a genuine conviction and speaks more *from* himself than *to* an audience. Such a speaker compels attention and does not exasperate where he strikes most relentlessly.

Cardinal Newman appreciated the weight added to an orator's words by the sense that he spoke not as an employed advocate, not as the mouthpiece of an institution, but from his life's experience. He said in the introduction to his discourses on *The Idea of a University* : —

"There are several reasons why I should open the discussion with a reference to the lessons with which past years have supplied me. One reason is this : It would concern me, Gentlemen, were I supposed to have got up my opinions for the occasion. This, indeed, would have been no reflection on me personally, supposing I were persuaded of their truth, when at length addressing myself to the inquiry ; but it would have destroyed, of course, the force of my testimony, and deprived such arguments, as I might adduce, of that moral persuasiveness which attends on tried and sustained conviction. It would have made me seem the advocate, rather than the cordial and deliberate maintainer and witness, of the doctrines which I was to support ; and though it might be said to evidence the faith I reposed in the practical judgment of the Church, and the intimate concurrence of my own reason with the course she had authoritatively sanctioned, and the devotion with which I could promptly put myself at her disposal, it would have cast suspicion on the validity of reasonings and conclusions which rested on no independent inquiry, and appealed to no past experience. In that case it might have been plausibly objected by opponents that I was the serviceable expedient of an emergency, and never, after all, could be more than ingenious and adroit in the management of an argument which was not my own, and which I was sure to forget again as readily as I had mastered it. But this is not so. The views to which I have referred have grown into my whole system of thought, and are, as it were, part of myself. Many changes has my mind gone through : here it has known no variation or vacillation of opinion, and though this by itself is no proof of the truth of my principles, it puts a seal upon conviction and is a justification of earnestness and zeal." — NEWMAN : *The Idea of a University.*

EXERCISES

1. Imagine yourself in the place of Major Rogers at the close of the French and Indian War, and translate the following paragraph into such an address as he might have made to the Indian chief Pontiac when the latter, unaware that the war was ended, tried to impede his progress on the way to Detroit : —

The war is over. The English have conquered the French, and I have come with my men to take possession of Detroit according to the terms of the treaty. If you will transfer your allegiance to the king of England, he will hold the French responsible for your previous enmity and grant you liberal terms of peace ; or, —

Suppose yourself in Thomas Jefferson's place when, during his ministry to France, he received a letter from his fifteen-year-old daughter Martha declaring her intention to become a nun. Tell what you think he must have said to her to induce her cheerfully to leave the convent school and go home with him to a life in which much of her father's comradeship, private tutors, and social gayety were the main features.

2. From what point of view is Becky's letter persuasive? Why does it fail?

" 'You will now, if you please, my dear, sit down at the writing-table and pen me a pretty little letter to Miss Crawley, in which you'll say that you are a good boy, and that sort of thing.' So Rawdon sate down, and wrote off, 'Brighton, Thursday,' and 'My dear aunt,' with great rapidity; but there the gallant officer's imagination failed him. He mumbled the end of his pen, and looked up in his wife's face. She could not help laughing at his rueful countenance, and marching up and down the room, with her hands behind her, the little woman began to dictate a letter, which he took down.

" ' Before quitting the country and commencing a campaign, which very possibly may be fatal — '

" 'What?' said Rawdon, rather surprised, but took the humour of the phrase, and presently wrote it down with a grin.

" ' Which very possibly may be fatal, I have come hither . . . . to say farewell to my dearest and earliest friend. I beseech you before I go, not perhaps to return, once more to let me press the hand from which I have received nothing but kindness all my life.'

" ' Kindness all my life,' echoed Rawdon, scratching down the words, and quite amazed at his own facility of composition.

"'I ask nothing from you but that we should part not in
anger. I have the pride of my family on some points,
though not on all. I married a painter's daughter, and am
not ashamed of the union.'

"'No, run me through the body if I am!' Rawdon
ejaculated.

"'You old booby,' Rebecca said, pinching his ear and
looking over to see that he made no mistakes in spelling —
'beseech is not spelt with an *a*, and earliest is.' So he
altered these words, bowing to the superior knowledge of
his little missis.

"'I thought that you were aware of the progress of my
attachment,' Rebecca continued; 'I knew that Mrs. Bute
Crawley confirmed and encouraged it. But I make no
reproaches. I married a poor woman, and am content to
abide by what I have done. Leave your property, dear
aunt, as you will. *I* shall never complain of the way in
which you dispose of it. I would have you believe that I
love you for yourself, and not for money's sake — I want to
be reconciled to you ere I leave England. Let me, let me
see you before I go. A few weeks or months hence it may
be too late, and I cannot bear the notion of quitting the
country without a kind word of farewell from you.'

"'She won't recognize my style in *that*,' said Becky. 'I
made the sentences short and brisk on purpose.'

  * * * * * * *

"Old Miss Crawley laughed when Briggs, with great mystery, handed her over this candid and simple statement.
'We may read it now Mrs. Bute is away,' she said. 'Read
it to me, Briggs.'

"When Briggs had read the epistle out, her patroness
laughed more. 'Don't you see, you goose,' she said to

Briggs, who professed to be much touched by the honest affection which pervaded the composition, — 'don't you see that Rawdon never wrote a word of it? He never wrote to me without asking for money in his life, and all his letters are full of bad spelling, and dashes, and bad grammar. It is that little serpent of a governess who rules him.' " — THACKERAY: *Vanity Fair*.

3. Select from literature good examples of persuasion.

4. Tell what you think Macaulay meant by each of the supporting propositions in the following bit of argument to prove Hume an " accomplished advocate."   Charged against a forensic writer, should you think the practices here enumerated praiseworthy or damaging, and why?

" Hume is an accomplished advocate; without positively asserting much more than he can prove, he gives prominence to all the circumstances which support his case; he glides lightly over those which are unfavorable to it; his own witnesses are applauded and encouraged; the statements which seem to throw discredit on them are controverted; the contradictions into which they fall are explained away; and a clear and connected abstract of their evidence is given; everything that is offered on the other side is scrutinized with the utmost severity; every suspicious circumstance is ground for comment and invective; what can not be denied is passed by without notice; concessions are sometimes made, but this insidious candor only increases the effect of the vast mass of sophistry." — T. B. MACAULAY: *History*.

5. Complete and pass in the forensic upon which you have been working.

RESEARCH

RESEARCH

A FORENSIC that is the result of "cramming" on one phase of a subject with which the writer is unfamiliar is apt to be ridiculous. A subject that requires research may, however, be treated with great profit to the student, and with a high degree of success, if the student makes intelligent and thorough preparation for his work. The preparation for such a paper is the most difficult and time-consuming part of the work, and for that reason a student in an English composition class can rarely afford to write papers that call for research.

An intelligent system will greatly help a student to economize effort. Attention should first be directed to getting into the atmosphere of the subject, so to speak, to acquiring such information as will make the student sympathetically at home in the subject; the second essential is to get a general background of information, so that he can regard the question not as isolated, but in its relation to other questions; the third and last step is to get thoroughly acquainted with and to collect evidence bearing on the specific question to be argued.

Where the question concerns measures or persons,

or events or places, or anything outside of the writer's range of experience, in order to escape giving it a wooden, dead treatment he must himself comprehend the question as a real and vital one.

To talk with those whose experience has touched upon or included the period, the place, the men, concerned, is an excellent way to attain this object. Half an hour's talk with such a man as Prince Kropotkin will give one more realization of the civil injustices existing in Russia than hours of diligent reading. If I had chosen a question pertaining to our own civil war, I should wish to talk with those who had actually felt the battle, with those whose dooryards had been battlefields, with the daughter of an Abolitionist who still thrills at the memory of five years spent in sustained elation of earnest devotion to a high principle; I should wish to talk with the man south of the Ohio who was burned in effigy and driven from town for voting for Lincoln, to the Copperhead on the northern shore who knew something of the dark plans of the Knights of the Golden Circle; I should like to turn over the old files of Horace Greeley's newspaper, to look over the war numbers of *Harpers' Weekly*, and read its editorials and war bulletins, look at its cartoons and caricatures of characters we suppose always to have been canonized.

Personal journals and letters contribute much towards making the past seem present, the remote seem near. The novelist or the dramatist often effectively transports one to strange scenes and untried conditions. If one would gain the point of view of those concerned in the industrial conflict of to-day, Charles Reade's *Put Yourself in his Place* and F. Hopkinson Smith's *Tom Grogan* present the "scab" as the victim of the "union"; Robert Herrick's *Web of Life* shows the "union" men as victims of the labor agitators; Henry James's *Princess Casamassima* and E. L. Voynich's *Olive Latham* show the agitators as victims of mistaken ideals.

The danger at this stage of the work is lest one should get prejudice rather than sympathy. If one would determine whether the private home was better than the large asylum for orphan children, it is not enough to see in Sudermann's drama, *The Fires of St. John*, the kindly-cared-for "calamity child's" craving for a bit of the true devotion she has discovered to exist and ready to gain it at any cost of her own honor or the happiness of others; it is not enough to read of the "private home" boy who considers himself handicapped for life, because he has missed the training that the institutional child can not escape — one should see as well the asylum children with their placid, dully content little faces.

The second step is to read around one's subject to get a background of knowledge for it; to see it not as an isolated unrelated unit; but to comprehend it in its right relation to other subjects. For example, it would be folly to try to treat the question of the *Subway Tavern's* prospect of success as a temperance measure without knowing about saloons in general, without knowledge of coffee-room and neighborhood-house experiments, without knowing the effect of stringent liquor laws, and attempts at total abstinence, without knowing the Bowery, and the statutes governing the sale of alcoholic liquors in New York. Of course, much of the knowledge gained on these kindred subjects will be of direct use in the argument.

When at last the student reaches the field that his question covers he still has important work to do. A hasty review of a few good magazine articles supporting the side he has decided to take will not suffice. He must read thoroughly on both sides of the question. It is always desirable to get at the source of information, to get back to the document from which most recent writers have drawn the evidence on which they have founded their conclusions. This is sometimes a very simple and valuable piece of work. Thus, nearly all the historic accounts of the work of Daniel Boone, nearly all the elaborate biographical treatises concerning him, have as their entire basis the brief and quaintly worded *Narrative* written by the old pioneer himself. But the original source, however valuable, is not enough. Men of old time were no more impeccable than men to-day ; and men of to-day of entire integrity of purpose often make serious mistakes in reporting occurrences. It is therefore indispensable that one should have also the benefit of the latest word on the subject, the benefit of the work of the wary and critical scholar who has discovered inconsistencies and mistakes.

Cross lights are also important. An historical subject has not been thoroughly investigated till the biographies of the history makers of the period have been studied; the literature, the art, the monuments, the maps of an epoch should be searched as witnesses.

As a rule it is bad economy to waste labor in doing over what has been done for one, but that is what we are most of the time doing in schools and colleges. Most large libraries have excellent card catalogues from which it is easy to make up a bibliography on almost any subject. Still, there are always times when such a catalogue is not available, and every student should know how to make a bibliography for himself. If one knows how to go about it, he may often serve himself better than the trained specialist will. A college debating team employed a specialist to make for them a list of references on the subject of their debate; but it was so long in coming that they set to work and made one for themselves that proved to be more complete and valuable than the one for which they paid ten dollars.

Poole's Index is, of course, the standard index for

periodic publications. In making a bibliography, first consult *Poole's Index*, looking up the various heads under which an article on the question might be catalogued. As soon as an article on your subject is found, make a note not only of it but of its author. Then look again through *Poole's Index* for articles by these authors — this time looking by authors instead of subjects. It is probable that if they are working on the subject and have published at all, they have published several articles, some of them under obscure titles that escaped your search by subjects. Having completed your search through all the volumes of *Poole's Index* both by subjects and authors and carefully noted all articles found, with authors, the student should next go to the *American Catalog* or to the index for the *Publishers' Trade List Annual*, which contains a list of the books published during recent years by nearly every publishing house in the country. Look up your subject by topics as before and take note of authors. Then look through the index for the authors you entered on your list, either from the index of the *Publishers' Trade List Annual* or from *Poole's Index* — the difference is that first you were looking for magazine articles, now you are looking for books. In the third place, you should, in like manner, look through the *Peabody Institute Catalogue* for books and pamphlets on the subject, that may now be out of print. You may further supplement your search by reference to *The A. L. A. Index to General Literature*, which is a guide to essays, reports, etc., published in collections and so not indexed in ordinary catalogues. *The A. L. A. Index to General Literature*, *Poole's Index*, the *American Catalog*, a *Publishers' Trade List Annual Index*, and a *Peabody Institute Catalogue* belong to the equipment of even the most limited college or public library.

At the start one should exert some ingenuity to think of possible cross reference. If one were discussing the removal of the Seminole Indians from Florida to land west of the Mississippi, one should look for Seminoles, Creeks, History of Alabama, History of Florida, Seminole War, Florida War, General Clinch, General Jackson, Osceola, and other Indian leaders, the maroons, runaway slaves, etc., for facts; Cooper, Helen Hunt Jackson, Jefferson, Irving, Parkman, etc., for atmosphere.

To read an important work on a subject (such as Sprague's *Florida War* on the subject just considered) and make note of persons, events, other works on the subject, that seem to the author to be of importance, is a good way to get a nucleus from which to start a bibliography.

Libraries, publishing houses, and old-book shops will furnish many of the books needed. In Mr. Harry Thurston Peck's *Life of Prescott* the following comparison occurs : —

"Irving resembled Livy in his use of authorities. Such sources as were ready to his hand and easy to consult he used with conscientious care : but those that were further afield, and for the mastery of which both time and labor were demanded, he let alone. . . . Compare these easy-going methods with the scientific thoroughness of Prescott, his ransacking, by agents, of every important library in Europe, his great collection of original documents, the many years which he gave to the study of them, and the conscientious judgment with which he weighed and balanced them. . . ."

The practical difficulties that prevent a student's getting at many of the valuable sources on his subject make it necessary that he should for the present content himself with the method of Irving, but it should always be with inner protest and with Prescott's method in mind as his ideal for his own future study.

It would be as undesirable as it would be impossible for the student to read all the articles and books he can obtain. He must early begin to cultivate a sense for an important document. Sometimes the reputation of a book or its author will enable him to rank it as reliable or worth while. But not all popular works are sound, and many works that are unknown to the student may be of the highest importance. He must, therefore, ultimately depend on his own judgment; he must read critically, cross-examining his witnesses as he goes, seeing that they sustain their assertions, that they take an impartial view, suppressing no damaging evidence and making no false charges; that they are sensible, exact, thorough, cautious, sure, genuine.

Even reliable works should not always be thoroughly read. The ability to "skip" intelligently, to pounce on the heart of a paragraph or chapter and take possession of it, is indispensable in research. The student must read with a sense of proportion, not lavishing time and strength on the beginning at such a rate that the end must be slighted. An enthusiastic beginning is always admirable, but to carry a thing through adequately is not less admirable.

While reading, the student should take such notes as he may wish to use in his argument. These should be concise and exact, with accurate references to author, title of book or article, page, volume, and publisher. This is important, as in a brief for an argument that requires research it is necessary definitely to note in the margin the source of whatever you cite as evidence.

INDEX

Important Text-Books in Rhetoric

BY ADAMS SHERMAN HILL
Boylston Professor of Rhetoric and Oratory in Harvard University

BEGINNINGS OF RHETORIC AND COMPOSITION . $1.25

This book is designed primarily to meet the needs of pupils in secondary schools who are learning to express themselves with the pen ; at the same time it contains so much information that is new in presentation and permanent in value that it is well adapted to more mature minds. Recognizing the fact that these needs can not be adequately supplied by treatises on the theory or the science of rhetoric, by cut and dried methods of instruction, or by diagrams, skeleton essays, or other mechanical devices, this work aims rather to stimulate the pupils to put their natural selves into all that they write. It helps them to remove the many obstacles that lie between thought and expression and shows the young writer how to present what he has to say in the best English within his reach and in the form best adapted to his purpose. No supplement with exercises is required in connection with this work, as the book is complete in itself. Nearly two hundred exercises are introduced to aid in the most practical way those who are traversing the ground between school grammar and advanced rhetoric.

FOUNDATIONS OF RHETORIC $1.00

The object of this book is to train boys and girls to say in written language, correctly, clearly, and effectively, what they have to say. It takes cognizance of faults such as those who are to use it are likely to commit, either from ignorance or from imitation of bad models, and of merits such as are within their reach. It gives a minimum of space to technicalities and a maximum of space to essentials. In language singularly direct and simple it sets forth fundamental principles of correct speaking, and accompanies each rule with abundant illustrations and examples, drawn from practical sources. It gives precisely the kind of training which young minds need to enable them to discriminate between good and bad forms of English.

PRINCIPLES OF RHETORIC $1.20

This popular work has been almost wholly rewritten, and is enlarged by much new material. The treatment is based on the principle that the function of rhetoric is not to provide the student of composition with materials for thought, nor yet to lead him to cultivate style for style's sake, but to stimulate and train his powers of expression—to enable him to say what he has to say in appropriate language. Deficiencies that time has disclosed have been supplied, the treatment of each topic adapted to present needs, and the book in its revised form has been made more serviceable.

AMERICAN BOOK COMPANY

THE MODERN MATHEMATICAL SERIES

FOR COLLEGES AND SECONDARY SCHOOLS

LUCIEN AUGUSTUS WAIT

General Editor

Senior Professor of Mathematics in Cornell University

ANALYTIC GEOMETRY
By J. H. Tanner, Ph.D., Assistant Professor of Mathematics, Cornell University, and Joseph Allen, A.M., Instructor in Mathematics in the College of the City of New York. Cloth, 8vo, 410 pages $2.00

DIFFERENTIAL CALCULUS
By James McMahon, A.M., Assistant Professor of Mathematics, Cornell University, and Virgil Snyder, Ph.D., Instructor in Mathematics, Cornell University. Cloth, 8vo, 351 pages $2.00

INTEGRAL CALCULUS
By D. A. Murray, Ph.D., Professor of Mathematics, Dalhousie College. Cloth, 8vo, 302 pages $2.00

DIFFERENTIAL AND INTEGRAL CALCULUS
By Virgil Snyder, Ph.D., Instructor in Mathematics, Cornell University, and John Irwin Hutchinson, Ph.D., Instructor in Mathematics, Cornell University. Cloth, 8vo, 320 pages $2.00

ELEMENTARY GEOMETRY—PLANE
By James McMahon, Assistant Professor of Mathematics in Cornell University. Half leather, 12mo, 358 pages, $0.90

ELEMENTARY ALGEBRA
By J. H. Tanner, Ph.D., Assistant Professor of Mathematics, Cornell University. Half leather, 8vo, 374 pages . . $1.00

ELEMENTARY GEOMETRY—SOLID
By James McMahon. (In preparation.)

ALGEBRA FOR COLLEGES
By J. H. Tanner. (In preparation.)

The advanced books of this series treat their subjects in a way that is simple and practical, yet thoroughly rigorous and atttactive to both teacher and student. They meet the needs of students pursuing courses in engineering and architecture in any college or university. The elementary books are designed to implant the spirit of the other books into secondary schools, and will make the work in mathematics, from the very start, continuous and harmonious.

AMERICAN BOOK COMPANY

Fisher's Brief History of the Nations

AND OF THEIR PROGRESS IN CIVILIZATION

By GEORGE PARK FISHER, LL.D.
Professor in Yale University.

Cloth, 12mo, 613 pages, with numerous Illustrations, Maps, Tables, and Reproductions of Bas-reliefs, Portraits, and Paintings. Price, $1.50

This is an entirely new work written expressly to meet the demand for a compact and acceptable text-book on General History for high schools, academies, and private schools. Some of the distinctive qualities which will commend this book to teachers and students are as follows:

It narrates in fresh, vigorous, and attractive style the most important facts of history in their due order and connection.

It explains the nature of historical evidence, and records only well established judgments respecting persons and events.

It delineates the progress of peoples and nations in civilization as well as the rise and succession of dynasties.

It connects, in a single chain of narration, events related to each other in the contemporary history of different nations and countries.

It gives special prominence to the history of the Mediaeval and Modern Periods, — the eras of greatest import to modern students.

It is written from the standpoint of the present, and incorporates the latest discoveries of historical explorers and writers.

It is illustrated by numerous colored maps, genealogical tables, and artistic reproductions of architecture, sculpture, painting, and portraits of celebrated men, representing every period of the world's history.

Copies of Fisher's Brief History of the Nations will be sent, prepaid, to any address on receipt of the price by the Publishers :

American Book Company

New York   •   Cincinnati   •   Chicago

Standard Text-Books in Physics

ROWLAND AND AMES'S ELEMENTS OF PHYSICS

By Henry A. Rowland, Ph.D., LL.D., and Joseph S. Ames, Ph.D., Professors of Physics in Johns Hopkins University.

Cloth, 12mo, 275 pages . . . . . Price, $1.00

This is designed to meet the requirements of high schools and normal schools, and is simple but logical and direct, being divided into two parts—the first treating of the theory of the subject, and the second containing suggestions to teachers.

AMES'S THEORY OF PHYSICS

By Joseph S. Ames, Ph.D.

Cloth, 8vo, 531 pages . . . . . . Price, $1.60

In this text-book, for advanced classes, the aim has been to furnish a concise and logical statement of the fundamental experiments on which the science of Physics is based, and to correlate these experiments with modern theories and methods.

AMES AND BLISS'S MANUAL OF EXPERIMENTS IN PHYSICS

By Joseph S. Ames, Ph.D., Professor of Physics, and William J. A. Bliss, Ph.D., Associate in Physics, in Johns Hopkins University.

Cloth, 8vo, 560 pages . . . . . . Price, $1.80

A course of laboratory instruction for advanced classes, embodying the most improved methods of demonstration from a modern standpoint, with numerous questions and suggestions as to the value and bearing of the experiments.

Copies sent, prepaid, to any address on receipt of price by the Publishers:

American Book Company

New York • Cincinnati • Chicago

Biology and Zoölogy

DODGE'S INTRODUCTION TO ELEMENTARY PRACTICAL BIOLOGY

A Laboratory Guide for High School and College Students. By CHARLES WRIGHT DODGE, M.S., Professor of Biology in the University of Rochester $1.80

This is a manual for laboratory work rather than a text-book of instruction. It is intended to develop in the student the power of independent investigation and to teach him to observe correctly, to draw proper conclusions from the facts observed, to express in writing or by means of drawings the results obtained. The work consists essentially of a series of questions and experiments on the structure and physiology of common animals and plants typical of their kind—questions which can be answered only by actual investigation or by experiment. Directions are given for the collection of specimens, for their preservation, and for preparing them for examination; also for performing simple physiological experiments.

ORTON'S COMPARATIVE ZOÖLOGY, STRUCTURAL AND SYSTEMATIC

By JAMES ORTON, A.M., Ph.D., late Professor of Natural History in Vassar College. New Edition revised by CHARLES WRIGHT DODGE, M.S., Professor of Biology in the University of Rochester $1.80

This work is designed primarily as a manual of instruction for use in higher schools and colleges. It aims to present clearly the latest established facts and principles of the science. Its distinctive character consists in the treatment of the whole animal kingdom as a unit and in the comparative study of the development and variations of the different species, their organs, functions, etc. The book has been thoroughly revised in the light of the most recent phases of the science, and adapted to the laboratory as well as to the literary method of teaching.

Copies of either of the above books will be sent, prepaid, to any address on receipt of the price.

American Book Company

New York • Cincinnati • Chicago

(167)

Scientific Memoir Series

EDITED BY JOSEPH S. AMES, Ph.D.

Johns Hopkins University

Copies sent, prepaid, to any address on receipt of the price.

American Book Company

New York   •   Cincinnati   •   Chicago
(183)

BOWNE'S THEISM

BY BORDEN P. BOWNE
Professor of Philosophy in Boston University

FOR COLLEGES AND THEOLOGICAL SCHOOLS

<u>PRICE, $1.75</u>

THIS BOOK is a revision and extension of the author's previous work, "Philosophy of Theism." In the present volume the arguments, especially from epistemology and metaphysics, receive fuller treatment. The work has been largely rewritten, and about half as much additional new matter has been included.

The author, however, still adheres to his original plan of giving the essential arguments, so that the reader may discern their true nature and be enabled to estimate their rational value. He does this from the conviction that the important thing in theistic discussion is not to make bulky collections of striking facts and eloquent illustrations, nor to produce learned catalogues of theistic writers and their works, but to clear up the logical principles which underlie the subject. From this point of view the work might rightly be called the "Logic of Theism."

Special attention is given to the fact that atheistic argument is properly no argument at all, but a set of illusions which inevitably spring up on the plane of sense-thought, and acquire plausibility with the uncritical. The author seeks to lay bare the root of these fallacies and to expose them in their baselessness. In addition, the practical and vital nature of the theistic argument is emphasized, and it is shown to be not merely nor mainly a matter of syllogistic and academic inference, but one of life, action, and history.

Copies sent, prepaid, on receipt of price

AMERICAN BOOK COMPANY
PUBLISHERS

NEW YORK   ·   CINCINNATI   ·   CHICAGO
(195)

A Descriptive Catalogue of High School and College Text-Books

WE issue a complete descriptive catalogue of our text-books for secondary schools and higher institutions, illustrated with authors' portraits. For the convenience of teachers, separate sections are published, devoted to the newest and best books in the following branches of study:

ENGLISH
MATHEMATICS
HISTORY AND POLITICAL SCIENCE
SCIENCE
MODERN LANGUAGES
ANCIENT LANGUAGES
PHILOSOPHY AND EDUCATION

If you are interested in any of these branches, we shall be very glad to send you on request the catalogue sections which you may wish to see. Address the nearest office of the Company.

AMERICAN BOOK COMPANY

Publishers of School and College Text-Books

NEW YORK	CINCINNATI	CHICAGO
BOSTON	ATLANTA	DALLAS	SAN FRANCISCO

(312)